PORTABLE
ARCHITECTURE

PORTABLE ARCHITECTURE

Design and Technology

Robert Kronenburg

Birkhäuser
Basel · Boston · Berlin

This book is a completely revised edition of "Portable Architecture".
The three previous editions were published in 1996, 2000, and 2003
by Architectural Press.

This book is also available in a German language edition
(ISBN 978-3-7643-8322-0).

Library of Congress Control Number: 2008921022

Bibliographic information published by the German National Library
The German National Library lists this publication in the Deutsche
Nationalbibliografie; detailed bibliographic data are available on the
Internet at http://dnb.d-nb.de.

© 2008 Birkhäuser Verlag AG
Basel · Boston · Berlin
P.O. Box 133, CH-4010 Basel, Switzerland
Part of Springer Science+Business Media

Printed on acid-free paper produced from chlorine-free pulp. TCF ∞

Layout: Esther Mildenberger, Brian Switzer, envision+,
www.envisionplus.com

Litho: Licht+Tiefe, Berlin

Printed in Germany

ISBN: 978-3-7643-8324-4

9 8 7 6 5 4 3 2 1
www.birkhauser.ch

Preface

When I first began this text I thought it would be primarily an update of my book *Portable Architecture*, last published in 2003. I was wrong. *Portable Architecture: Design and Technology* can be assessed as a new book in its own right with a new structure and new content that more tightly focuses on its aim, which is to study and compare significant contemporary examples of portable architecture in order to establish the crucial characteristics that make it successful.

In a built environment that is now affected more and more by rapid and dramatic change, ecological considerations, and social and cultural impact, a form of architecture that is flexible, lightweight in construction, has minimal impact on sensitive sites, and is responsive to new technological and aesthetic opportunities has great value. This book places examples of good portable architectural design in context with each other, examines the common elements that have led to their creation, and thereby discovers the factors that have been critical to their success. Analysis of these factors will be of interest to those involved in the design and manufacture of buildings (not necessarily all of which are portable) where similar issues are important. It may also result in further work that identifies valuable directions for future building projects and architectural research. The projects described here dispel preconceptions that mobile buildings are mainly low-cost, short-life products and confirm that the building type is an important part of mainstream architectural development. They show that mobile buildings are feasible, are able to fulfil many different roles, and are economically viable to build and operate.

The genre of transportable, mobile, and ephemeral architecture is not only continuously changing but is also expanding. Though it has been necessary to include some of the projects from the earlier book because of their importance in the field, their descriptions have been revised, updated, and rewritten. For the first time I have had to make difficult decisions about which projects to leave out. In most cases this decision has been made on the basis of their age, and the fact that they have been covered elsewhere, often in my own books. In selecting the projects I have tried to cover the full range of approaches to making portable architecture that exists in the world today, so although there may be some buildings not examined in detail, there are others that utilise a similar strategy to achieve their aim. Like its predecessor, *Portable Architecture: Design and Technology* is still the only book that takes a case study approach to the examination of these buildings, exploring in detail the strategies and tactics employed by clients, designers, and builders to achieve the objective of creating a quality environment, which nevertheless is mobile. Because of its concentration on detail, preparing this book would not have been possible without the cooperation and generosity of those who have commissioned, designed, and built the buildings examined in the case studies. I must therefore express my gratitude to those who have helped with my research by giving their time and material – in particular Mike Ball, Mark Fisher, Nick Goldsmith, Richard Horden, Theo Jansen, David Kelsall, Giusseppe Lignano, Ada Tolla, to fruition.

Robert Kronenburg
University of Liverpool – April 2008

Introduction

Portable buildings have been in use since humankind first began to build, yet because of their impermanent nature it is only comparatively recently that they have begun to be perceived as architecture. Traditional architecture has been reevaluated and buildings previously labelled as 'primitive' are now recognised for their finely tuned response to environmental, social, and cultural conditions and as precursors to later, more sophisticated architectural forms. Familiar traditional building forms such as the tent, tipi, and yurt utilise sophisticated constructional techniques and complex habitation patterns that have not only retained their relevance for thousands of years but are linked to some of the most sophisticated building patterns of the present day. The Bedouin tent incorporates compressive struts and tensile membranes that utilise the same principles as modern tensile engineering systems. The North American tipi can be compared to a single cell of a space frame, adapted to use membranes without inherent strength (animal hides) and incorporating twin skin systems and natural air movement patterns for environmental modification. The Asian yurt uses modular manufacturing techniques and a geodesic-based wall structure that are familiar twentieth century constructional strategies. Contemporary portable buildings have a long and valuable pedigree, which includes principles that have been adapted for permanent construction.

Portable architecture consists of structures that are intended for easy erection on a site remote from their manufacture. The term 'portable' has been used as a general description for movable buildings for nearly two centuries: in 1830 John Manning, a London carpenter and builder, conceived a prefabricated timber building that could be packaged into a small volume for transportation overseas and called it the 'Manning Portable Colonial Cottage'. Between 1895 and 1940 many thousands of mail order homes such as the 'Sears Simplex Portable Cottage' were transported and erected throughout North America.

The simplest 'portable' strategy consists of buildings that are transported in one piece for instant use once they arrive at their location. Some incorporate their transportation method into their permanent structure and may be built on a chassis or a hull. Such buildings are generally restricted in size due to the limitations of transport, though not always – the Barrier Reef Floating Hotel is a

1   2

1/2 The Wanderer, 1895. Built by
Dr. William Gordon Stables and believed to
be the first purpose-built leisure caravan.

200 bedroom building that incorporates a restaurant, kitchen, shops, disco, and bars. A more common strategy that also enables greater variety in built form is the building constructed from factory-made elements transported as a partly complete package and then quickly assembled at the site. The third type of portable building is composed of a system of modular parts that are easily transportable and usually dry assembled on site. This method allows maximum flexibility for adaptation to different layouts; however, it also usually requires a more complex assembly procedure carried out by a larger erection team over a longer period. These three basic strategies can be used with many alternative constructional systems that incorporate panel, framed, tensile, and pneumatic structural principles, sometimes in combination, to create an infinite variety of built forms. The design of portable buildings is not restricted by the lack of construction options, which enables them to range in size and complexity from a Portaloo to a 10,000 seat auditorium.

The term 'architecture' is used in recognition of the fact that many contemporary portable building examples have an equally significant effect on the built environment as static structures. There is hardly a field of human activity that they do not support in some way – housing, education, medicine, commerce, manufacture, entertainment, and military operations are a few. However, a common perception of the contemporary portable building is that it is primarily a standard product such as the mobile home or site hut, and its presence within the building industry is peripheral – useful in the same way as a piece of machinery or a tool. The majority of small-scale applications are commercially manufactured, loose-fit products, which are acquired for their speed of deployment and are not dedicated to their purpose nor specifically tuned to the activities they support. Though such standard products have their uses, they have very little in common with the ambitious projects described in this book. These use sophisticated construction technology to achieve impressive operational standards that fulfil diverse functions. In these significant projects, the portability of the building has been an especially important factor in the design requirements and sufficient lead-in time has been available for the creation of a dedicated solution. The mobile element in these projects' design has not only been the driving force in the creation of their form and image, but also an important factor in their operational success.

Though portable building should be understood as a part of all architecture, its realisation does not always derive from conventional circumstances. There is a wide diversity in its form and function, which has resulted in a problem-solving approach to design. Portable architecture is a field of great variety and of interconnections – influences and experience can be identified not only with many different areas of architecture but also vehicle, product, and materials development. In many cases specialist expertise has been developed both inside and outside the building industry during collaborative exploration between designers and manufacturers in order to resolve the issues of a specific project.

Each of the design teams involved in the projects studied here have generally worked independently of each other, however, there are some interesting common factors. One example is the way that engineering expertise in specialist lightweight building systems has been shared – engineers Ove Arup, Atelier One, Whitby and Bird, and Buro Happold have all worked with various leading architects and designers on portable building projects. Many of the design teams are also involved in more mainstream work for permanent structures and perceive their portable building design experience as an area of expertise that informs and is informed by architectural design in general. The functional operation of architectural spaces and facilities clearly benefits from the expertise of those who are professional building designers, however, the design teams also appear to have had little difficulty adjusting to the very different budgeting arrangements for portable architecture. Building costs may only be a small part of a package that also includes transportation and operation, and constructional arrangements that may include builders and material and component manufacturers who do not usually work within the construction industry.

There can be no doubt that society is passing through a period of great change. Technological, economic, and political shifts across the world are dramatically altering the way our built environment is shaped. There are many predictions of how the future will develop – few envision utopia, many foresee distopia. Most believe, however, that one thing will remain constant, and that is change! In fact, change is crucial if the world is to be saved from complete and dramatic network breakdown, particularly in environmental terms. Many influential design professionals and commentators believe that flexibility and adaptability is

an intrinsic component of a forward-looking design agenda. Contemporary architecture has now to respond to significant influences that were deemed relatively unimportant until recently. Ecological considerations that measure the use of renewable resources, recyclable components, and building costs on a life-cycle basis are now enormously significant. The societal impact of development, particularly in urban areas, is now a dominant factor as is the context of sensitive and historic sites. These pressures are reflected in the resulting restrictions placed on building design by planning and construction controls and other legislation. Economic pressure on the building industry now results in fast track programmes for higher specification buildings built with fewer skilled personnel.

Portable architecture may be able to aid in the development of an industry-wide strategy that involves new materials, components, and building methods. As a type of building design that must respond to relatively extreme operational parameters it more often makes use of experimental and exploratory logistical and constructional methods that may ultimately have more general value. Connections that exist between the portable building projects described in this book already indicate that there is a pattern of new phenomena that deserve further investigation. The expertise and experience of those normally not involved with the building industry is also of value in the development of new architectural solutions and it is in cross-over design areas like this that such benefits can first be appreciated. Designing for mobile solutions should therefore not be seen as some unique hybrid manifestation, part way between transport and building design. It is without doubt a facet of mainstream architectural design. This can be justified for a number of reasons, some pragmatic and others more philosophical. All good portable architecture sets out to create an identifiable sense of place in exactly the same way as a permanent building does. The fact that its physical existence on a particular site may be subject to dramatic erection and dismantling procedures and be comparatively limited in time also adds a sense of excitement associated with event and performance. This phenomenon may be compared with the accelerated motion of a speeded-up film which provides a fascinating view that compresses a process that normally takes much longer. No matter how long the building is present on a particular site, for that period the portable building's primary function remains the same as a similar permanent facility – to support the

3

4

3 The Markies mobile dwelling
designed by architect Eduard Bhötlingk,
Netherlands, 1995.
4 Mobile home on the road, Kansas, USA.

activities that are accommodated. The way in which it achieves this should not be compromised by its portability and the user should not have to suffer inferior standards simply because the building happens to be movable. Many standard products stress their instant availability as a key factor in their marketing and expect clients to compromise their performance standards for this benefit. The good designer approaches the task of creating permanent or portable architecture with the same set of priorities, balancing all the factors pertinent to the project. Portability is just another factor like lighting, security, or access arrangements. Designer or client may decide that the portable element in the design brief may provide the opportunity for the creation of a specific image associated with movement, but it may equally be one of stability and continuity that is required. All portable buildings should therefore be judged by the same criteria as other architecture – fitness for purpose, appropriate for context, beautiful in form, economy in use.

Because of the particular circumstances of their erection, portable buildings are generally composed of relatively lightweight materials. This is a characteristic

that can be traced from vernacular and traditional examples through to the latest computer-aided designs that are made in factories. In general, materials are expressed in their construction because to disguise them is to add unnecessary complexity and additional weight. This also applies to their structural composition, which enables a clear identification of the difference between supporting elements and cladding elements. Well-designed portable buildings exhibit clarity of architectural expression that makes them exemplars of functional form generation, and they therefore occupy a place at the forefront of architectural design development. This reinforces the reason why portable architecture is part of the mainstream – the methods of construction and techniques of manufacture it pioneers are applicable to all types of building. The use of lightweight, prefabricated, componentised construction can reduce site work, building time, and transportation costs. New building methods originally devised for demountable buildings have been transferred to permanent constructional operations – components developed for a primary market in permanent buildings are now being used in portable structures. It is therefore clear

5

6

5 Winnebago Brave travel home,
Arizona, USA.
6 Airstream Europe Model 534. A new
version of the archetypal mobile home
designed specifically for European roads.

that the study of the design, manufacture, construction, and operation of this particular architectural field has potential benefits in all.

However, there is a lack of coordinated research activity into portable building techniques. Industry-led research is primarily legislation led and concentrates on increasing the standards in existing products to meet more stringent statutory requirements. The introduction of user-led research could lead to the development of new markets and applications. Innovative one-off designs like most of those described here are a valuable research resource in that practical examples of working structures can be used as models for future investigation. Experimental projects that have the purpose of paving the way for new forms of design are an accepted part of many industries' research and development strategy, particularly those where innovation is the key to maintaining the competitive edge – for example aerospace, motor racing, or information technology. In architecture, full-scale building to perform this task is extremely rare – individual component manufacturers will prototype their own products, organisations such as the Building Research Establishment will construct

mock-ups to test performance and safety, but the creation of an entirely new building in which all the elements are part of a new inter-related approach to building design, manufacture, and construction is something that the building industry, composed as it is of a network of inter-twined yet competitive organisations, cannot undertake. Occasionally, 'experimental' buildings have featured in specialist exhibitions or as part of commercial expos, however, there is often a hidden agenda with such projects, the experimentation intended to draw attention to their sponsor, rather than to seriously attempt to explore the limits of a genuinely innovative concept. It is therefore not surprising that the experimental buildings examined here have often been created outside the conventions of the construction industry. Though they are clearly architecture, they stand outside the normal world of the building industry due to their unique commissioning, design, construction, and operational characteristics.

In some cases the expertise of professional designers is already being utilised by parts of the manufacturing industry (marquee tent manufacturers employ Buro Happold in the UK and FTL Design Engineering Studio in the USA) and this is an optimistic sign for future develop-ment. The objectives of a coordinated industry-based research programme would be to improve the image of the portable building, to communicate its advantages, and develop its potential. This will not be easy – the difficulties of transferring research into application is reinforced by many projects which have been successful in prototype but failed to make it into large-scale production. Buckminster Fuller's 1946 low-cost, factory-made Wichita House had 37,000 advance orders placed though only two prototypes were ever made. However, the examples described in this book convincingly indicate the potential of portable architecture – a potential to be both the best architecture and the best engineering.

Most of the buildings described here have been com-missioned by clients who are unsure what they actually want, though they have a clear idea of what they want to do – instead of saying they want a 'building', they may say they want an 'exhibition', or an 'experience', or a 'shelter'. The designer has therefore been placed in a much more powerful role than usual – as well as advising on architec-tural form and construction he or she may also be deter-mining operational criteria and siting.

The nature of commissioning is also different, utilising much less formal contracts based on performance-related goals rather than strict provisions of space, volume, and environment. Rather than a desire to get the most space for the least cost there is an understanding that the achievement of the facility's goals within an acceptable budget is the prime objective. In addition, operational costs are often taken as a part of the budget – energy, transportation, maintenance, erection, and dismantling costs emerging as equally important elements in a pre-determined cost package. It is also of interest that though contracts are far less involved, the actual projects are frequently far more complex and incorporate many more variables than in conventional building. Nevertheless, in the case studies described here the performance criteria stipulated in the contract have usually been exceeded – the building costing less to operate than originally forecast, capable of speedier erection, and having a longer life or secondary use beyond the parameters of the initial brief. The clients received more for their money thanks to the ingenuity of the designer and the skills of the builder.

Portable architecture is as varied in form and image as mainstream building, however, some common factors can be perceived and these relate primarily to materiality. Though its image does not fall into a set visual pattern,

there is one factor that is common to most designs – these buildings seem to represent something new. This may be explained by the understandable recourse of designers to light and strong materials which are best suited to the requirements of transportation and demountability – the lightest, strongest construction methods consist of comparatively high technology systems.

Even when the designer's ambition has been specif-ically to create a portable building that has the presence of high-quality architecture (rather than high-quality temporary building) the image created is still one of lightweight, modern efficiency. Membranes are becoming increasingly common in either tensioned form or as air-supported structures. This is not only because increased performance and longer life can be expected from the new range of membranes but also because of the relative ease with which they can now be manipulated at the design stage due to computer-aided design. Architects can create three-dimensional forms in physical or com-puter-generated models, which can then be transferred to programmes that carry out the detailed stress cal-culations and pattern making. Advances continue to be made not only in the creation of new products like ETFE foils and elastomers, but also in the development of well-proven materials like canvas. Perhaps the traditional image of the tent membrane as the classic portable shelter has helped reinforce its new role in making architecture.

Plastics such as glass reinforced polyester, fibreglass, epoxies, and polycarbonates are being used in a wide range of other roles besides membranes, for pultrusions, jointing, tension lines, webbing, windows, doors, and rigid panels. Aluminium and steel remain the most common compression member materials for their availability and familiarity in component manufacture. Where costs allow or performance dictates, new advanced technology materials such as carbon fibre and Kevlar are being intro-duced. These spin-offs from other advanced industries inevitably surface first in building designs that have high performance requirements combined with the necessity to retain low weight.

Advances in control systems are also now affecting portable building designs, making possible self-levelling mechanisms, hydraulically and pneumatically operated components, self-deploying structures, and self-monitor-ing and responsive envelopes and environments. These systems, once restricted to static, permanently located machinery, have now become sufficiently robust, compact, and economic in their use of energy to be portable.

Despite these inevitable technological advances, many of which find their first use in the creation of portable architecture, such buildings do not exist just because the new technology is now available to make them. Buildings that move from place to place have been designed, made, and used for millennia. The need for portable buildings is what drives the demand for them – the fact that they can now be made more easily or more efficiently simply makes them more attractive when the alternative is a wasteful disposable building. It has been suggested that the building industry does not need any more new materials or techniques at all, what it really needs to do is build better with the old ones. Traditional portable buildings have frequently used commonplace materials such as timber, cord, cloth, or felt to create sophisticated, environmentally aware, finely tuned buildings. Most contemporary designers have a natural inclination to explore the potential of the latest, lightest, most modern products in order to achieve their goals. Frequently, when the budget does not allow these materials to be included, they have been forced to use more prosaic methods – plywood, standard steel sections, rope, canvas, etc. Sometimes they perceive this as a failure or a compromised solution, however, the cheapest, most commonplace materials, free materials, or those which have been repeatedly recycled, can also make wonderful spaces and forms – for example, polythene sheet containing water for foundations, unprocessed wood for walls, and air under pressure for a roof. Where the building use is temporary, the siting of limited duration, and the impact transient, experimentation is as valuable for an innovative low-tech building as it is for a high-tech one.

An important reason for preparing this book is that the successful manufacture of a high-quality building that can move from place to place is a remarkable achievement that deserves detailed examination and communication to a wider audience. Architects, engineers, and manufacturers who have undertaken these genuinely innovative building projects have attempted to meet head on the issues of demanding briefs that require unprecedented performance levels from buildings that move. However, the remarkable standard of technical and operational performance that is sometimes achieved has in many cases been ignored, media coverage tending to explore the novelty value of such projects rather than the lessons they may hold for the industry at large. This is understandable as portable buildings are of interest in the same way that a prototype car design is of interest – it is a manifestation of contemporary technology to which most people can easily relate. It has

a dynamic quality that is of the moment, and imagery that is in turn stimulating and seductive. However, portable building design is different to 'this year's model' in an important way, no matter what the manufacturer's blurb might say – the prime motivations in car design are style and fashion, the prime motivations in building design (though not excluding style, fashion, or many other cultural aspirations) are function and continuity. The strategies and techniques which are new to the construction industry and make portable architecture so interesting in its own right can be tested out here before use in more general situations – the role of such innovation is to enable the design and manufacture of more appropriate, more efficient, more economic architecture that better serves all functions, both temporary and permanent.

For the designers who work in the field of portable architecture there are no boundaries in the sources of inspiration between mobile and static design. The transfer of concepts between temporary and permanent architecture is an accepted and commonplace part of their design process. The introduction of new types of procurement and construction procedures and the use of manufacturers in different industries are challenging the way that the traditional building industry operates. These designers are invariably knowledgeable about other fields that impact on their own and have built up a network of professional consultants, specialist manufacturers, and constructors who have developed the expertise and resources to solve new problems. Their energy, confidence, and skill are remarkable and it is clear from the projects described here that their work is expanding the thresholds of building design.

7

7 Oil Rig, Cromarty Scotland –
a mobile industrial facility.
8 Inflate Air Camper – a prototype
fast response shelter designed to
challenge the standard camping tent.

8

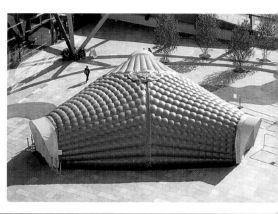

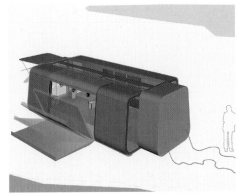

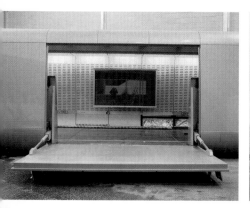

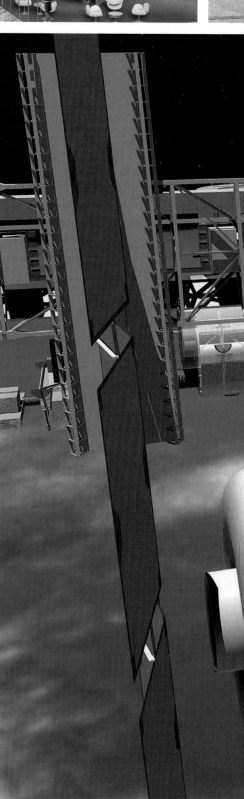

Renzo Piano Building Workshop
IBM Travelling Pavilion

1982–1984
Architect: Renzo Piano Building Workshop, Genoa, Italy;
Renzo Piano, Shunji Ishida, Alessandro Traldi
Engineer: Ove Arup & Partners, London, UK;
Peter Rice, Tom Barker
Client: IBM Europe

One of the most significant advantages of portable architecture is the capability to be sited in important and sensitive locations. The advantages to commercial clients who wish to communicate the qualities of their products and services to as many people as possible are clear. These exhibition and public relations events can take advantage of prominent locations and prestigious sites, albeit temporarily. The advantage for the development of modern architecture is that it is seen in relation to other types of buildings in a favourable way, both responding to the natural environment and acting as a foil to its historic, man-made setting. Buildings of quality such as this prove that modern architecture can possess distinct, quantifiable advantages that if used appropriately is suitable for many settings and applications.

Renzo Piano has described his primary architectural concern as 'the method of making buildings', and his design practice, the Building Workshop, explores a holistic integration of materials, techniques, and programmes to guide their formal and logistical approach in the creation of architecture. Piano's best known early building is the Centre Georges Pompidou, built in Paris between 1971 and 1977 and designed in partnership with Richard Rogers and engineer Peter Rice. Piano's subsequent architecture has been diverse and is characterised by the distinctive thematic differences that have shaped each individual project. However, a common philosophy can be perceived – there is a persistent technological approach that exploits the opportunities of contemporary materials and techniques in partnership with traditional or conventional systems so that all may be used to best advantage.

Piano has been involved in design activities outside the field of conventional architecture including sailing yachts, cars, trucks, and even two cruise ships for P&O Ferries. He has also been involved in many projects for experimental, temporary, and transportable architecture, from high-budget cultural buildings like the Italian Industry Pavilion at the Osaka Expo of 1970 to the minimal-cost Magic Box disaster relief project in 1985. The former was designed to express the sophisticated technological capabilities of Italian industrial production; the latter was a rapid intervention communications and monitoring facility unit for disaster situations based on Piano's experience with UNESCO in Third World countries.

1

2

3

1   IBM pavilion and one of its service vehicles.
2/3   Mobile buildings can utilise famous
landmarks as a temporary 'address' – the IBM
pavilion here in Paris and Rome.

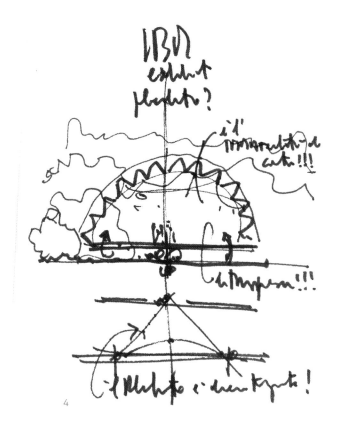

4

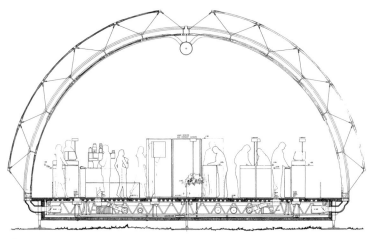

5

The Building Workshop's most influential mobile building project has been the exhibition pavilion created for IBM's tour of European cities between 1982 and 1984. The brief was to create a venue that would communicate the developing power of computer technology in a direct, hands-on way. The IBM travelling pavilion was intended to communicate the quality and usability of their computers and to take advantage of parkland sites in city centres – the image was of a close-to-nature building that contained the latest technological equipment. This apparent dichotomy counteracted the then common perception of computers being tools for specialist use, and generated one of the most interesting aspects of the designers' solution. How could a building convey the high-technology characteristics of its contents whilst directly relating to elements in nature, and still accommodate the complex constructional problems of a completely portable structure?

Renzo Piano worked with Building Workshop partner Shunji Ishida and Ove Arup engineer Peter Rice to create a solution that responded to these complex issues. The pavilion consisted of an 85 metre long, 480 square metre semi-circular tube that contained all the servicing required

for it to operate independent of a mains supply, day and night. The structure was based on a suspended steel floor that contained a hollow space for services. To this was attached a series of free-standing three-pin arches fixed to the edge of the floor at their base. The two segments of each arch consisted of an ingenious structural system that incorporated traditional and modern mater-ials used in conjunction to provide an organic yet technological image. Each segment consisted of six polycarbonate pyra-mids (manufactured and fitted in units of three) fixed at the point and the rim by cast aluminium joints to laminated timber (larch) booms. These transparent pyr-amids therefore formed not only the structural connection that made up the arch but also the skin of the building. Neoprene gaskets and adjustable stainless steel rods were used at connection points to allow for differential movement between the various materials, and also to accommodate the flexibility required in the setting up and dismantling of a portable building.

23 bright yellow IBM trucks customised by the project fabricators and erection team, Calabrese Engineering, were used to transport the facility. 21 contained the building

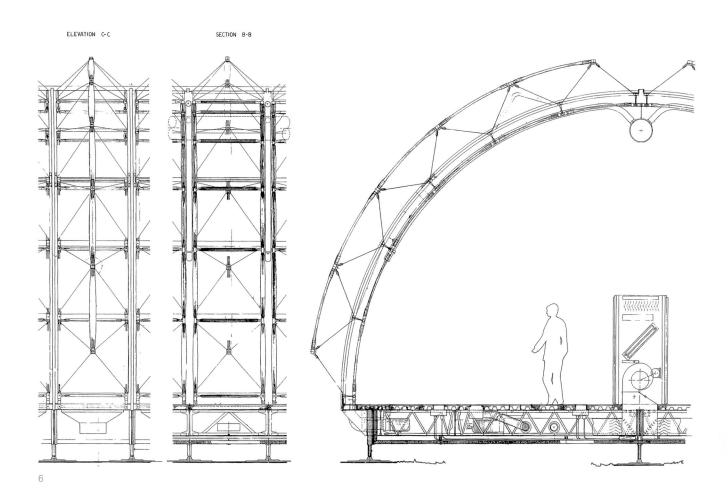

ELEVATION C-C   SECTION B-B

6

4/5 Design sketch and cross-section.
6 Detailed cross-section and part
elevation, IBM pavilion. The sub-floor
area contains services including ducts
to the central air-conditioning unit.

components and internal equipment and two contained
the mainframe computer and air-conditioning system.
A forklift truck, hired separately at each location, moved
the components into position. The steel floor structure was
erected on adjustable feet, and the arches were assembled
on a working surface laid out near the site. One segment
of each arch was connected at its bottom edge to the floor
and the top edge elevated into position with a pneumatic
tool. The other segment was fixed at its bottom edge and
its top edge elevated to meet the opposite part at the top.
As the building stayed in each location for up to two months,
site preparations were often made which included ramps,
landscaping, and approach paths.

Because of the delicate equipment the pavilion contained, environmental control was important and it therefore incorporated a number of passive and active control
features. Opaque insulating panels made from Perspex
with separate aluminium mesh shades could be fixed into
the polycarbonate pyramids. These were supplemented
by tensile shading membranes that hung within the space
and reduced glare on the computer screens. Active environmental modification consisted of air-conditioning units

placed down the centre of the building. Condensation
was prevented from forming on the skin by pumping warm
air down a central duct beneath the apex and distributing
it against the arch walls using aircraft-type nozzles pointed
at the polycarbonate pyramids. The entire exhibition could
be erected in three weeks and, as with other travelling
performance events, two separate structures were made
so that one could be serviced whilst the other was in use.

The success of the IBM pavilion was such that four
times the number of people predicted visited it at each
site. Its importance in terms of influence was that it challenged the idea that temporary buildings have to be simple
and concentrate so much of their budget into solving
pragmatic assembly and deployment problems that there
is nothing left to make the architecture. Despite its significant presence as a building, it can also appropriately
be perceived as a piece of sophisticated product design –
an object that crosses boundaries between different
applications. The building became an exhibition tool in
itself, displaying the concerns of the manufacturer as well
as the products within.

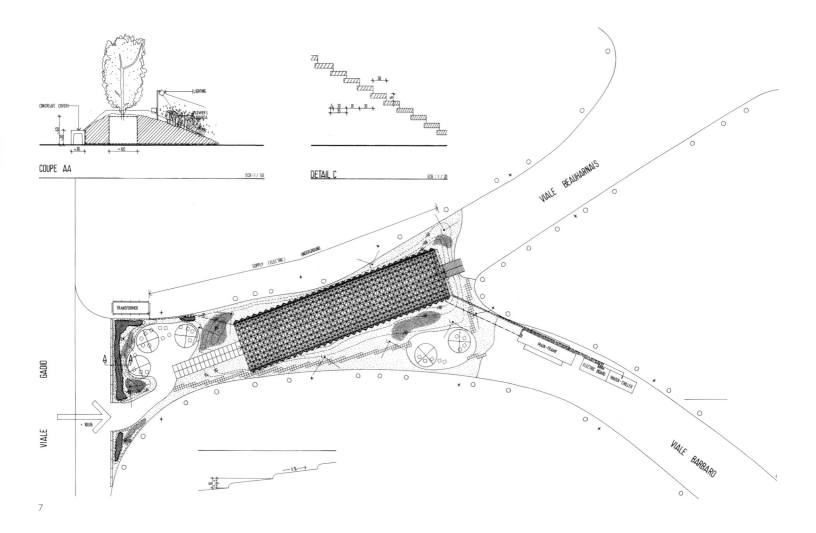

COUPE AA   ECH :1 / 50   DETAIL C   ECH :1 / 20

7

The pavilion was a man-made form designed to complement the natural landscape. It merged into its sites to a certain degree because of its cellular, organic form and reflective skin, however, there is no doubt that its dominant image was as an example of contemporary technologically based design. The modular nature of its construction was clearly expressed in its form and utilised in its erection and manufacture, yet this did not result in a mechanistic, repetitive structure but one that used the contrast of solidity and transparency to reflect natural light and the external features of the site. The positioning of this sensitively designed visitor to historic sites adjacent to the Natural History Museum in London, the Eiffel Tower in Paris, and the Castello Sforzesco in Milan resulted in dynamic and stimulating contrasts not usually found in the built environment.

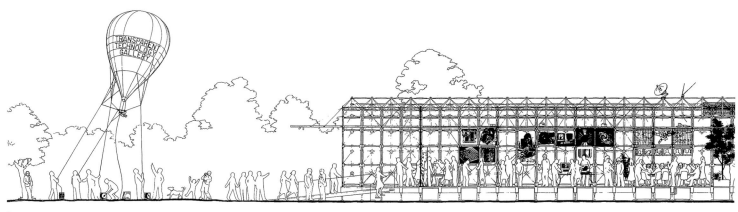

8

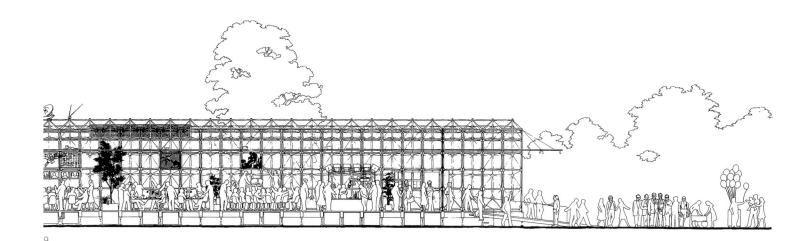

9

7 Typical site layout drawing.
8/9 Long section, IBM pavilion.

Shigeru Ban

Japan Pavilion

Nomadic Museum

Shigeru Ban is famous for his design work involving unconventional materials, in particular paper, but also bamboo and recycled substances. However, he also has an exceptional approach to the possibilities of creating particularly adaptable architectural forms. The novelty and exploration he brings to the use of materials he also brings to the detailed design of his buildings, even if they are made from standard constructional approaches. He describes his design ideology as against waste and for invention.

Ban believes that he recognised his approach to architectural design during a high school project in which he was asked to make different structures from a variety of materials including paper, bamboo, and wood. Later, after studying architecture at the Cooper Union School in New York City, he discovered the discarded material of the paper tube, using it first in his exhibition design for the Alvar Aalto exhibit at the Museum of Modern Art in 1986. Though acceptable for an exhibition design, the use of paper tubes as a building material was problematic because they had not been tested for this purpose. Eventually, beginning with the Odawara Festival Hall and Gate in 1990, Ban was able to build a significant building using 8 metre long tubes.

Japan Pavilion

2000
Architect: Shigeru Ban Architects, Tokyo, Japan, and Frei Otto, Leonberg, Germany
Consultants: Buro Happold Engineers, Bath, UK

Despite the inevitable result of an international exhibition being extensive construction and transportation costs, the theme of Expo 2000 in Hanover, Germany, was the environment. Shigeru Ban was invited to design the Japan Pavilion and decided that it was especially important to take a sustainable approach in building a structure that would only have a temporary existence at that site. His goal was to create a building that could be completely dismantled, with all the elements from which it was made being capable of being reused in similar or different forms – either reused or recycled. Collaborating with the famous innovator of tension grid shell structures, Frei Otto, Ban was inspired to propose a grid shell using paper tubes. The form would be in the shape of a tunnel arch that undulated along its length – the changes in width and height making

1

2

1 Japan Pavilion, Hanover Expo 2000,
Germany. Exterior of the pavilion showing
the bamboo main structure.
2 Interior view.

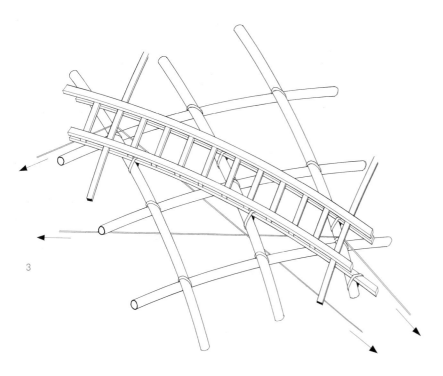

3

4

it stronger by aiding lateral restraint. A secondary structural layer of slender wooden ladder arches was suggested by Otto to further stiffen the structure but also to provide a fixing point for the external roof membrane, which was also to be paper-based. The manufacturers of waterproof paper bags developed this membrane, and although it was tested and proven acceptable in performance terms, it was necessary to add an additional plastic layer in response to German Building Authority requirements. The tube grid joints were made from simple building tape. Metal node points were also fixed to the arches and diagonal cables used to brace the entire free span structure which was 74 metres long by 25 metres wide by 16 metres high. The end walls consisted of timber arches with metal cables tensioned at a 60° angle like a tennis racquet to support a triangulated honeycomb paper grid. The main space was left open so that the delicate latticework of the structure could be appreciated against the translucent paper skin. The foundations were made from a steel framework filled with sand boxes made from reusable shuttering boards. Loose laid stone aggregates and reusable containers were also incorporated into the

completely recyclable facility, which took a total of three weeks to erect on site. After the Expo the structural paper tubes were bought and recycled by a German paper tube company and the honeycomb paper end panels were reused as interior partitions.

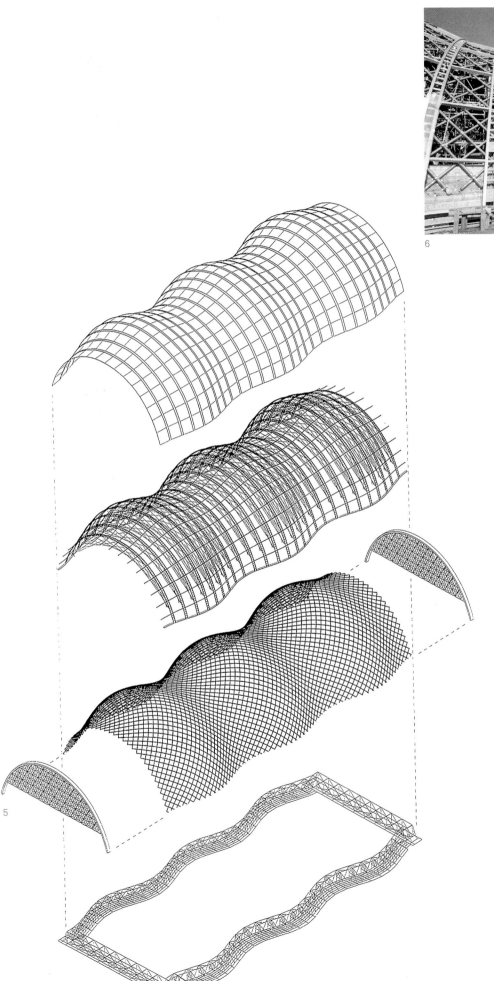

3 Diagram showing the structural system.
4 Assembly process showing the layered
construction.
5 Exploded axonometric.
6 Timber secondary structure that
supports the paper membrane.

1

Nomadic Museum

2005–2007
Architect: Shigeru Ban Architects, Tokyo, Japan
Client: Gregory Colbert, The Rolex Institute

It is not always necessary to move all the components of a building when it is rebuilt in another location – a particularly valuable strategy to consider if the building is large. Key components can be relocated whilst the main elements are carefully selected for their availability at all the proposed sites. One such component is the standard ISO shipping container. In 2005, Shigeru Ban was asked to create a mobile art exhibition space for international photographic artist Gregory Colbert. Colbert exhibits large photographic portraits of people communing with animals. Colbert exhibited the work from his Ashes and Snow show at the Venice Biennale in 2002 and it was bought in its entirety by a dedicated collector who then encouraged him to tour the work to other cities. Ban had the idea of using objects that would be found in every location that the show would travel to and the container was an obvious choice.

It was also chosen as a vessel in which to transport the exhibits, which are shipped in 14 containers between the global exhibition sites.

The first site was on Manhattan Pier 54 on the Hudson River in New York City. 148 empty ISO containers were stacked by a floating crane into a self-supporting grid to form the main building envelope. Other less substantial walls are made with wire-braced fabric. Aluminium rafters braced by cables support a PVC membrane roof surface. This structure is supported by paper tube and steel cable trusses supported on twin paper columns 10 metres high. Erection begins with the stacking of the containers in a carefully measured layout on the site. The rafters are then craned into position and the triangular paper tube roof braces positioned below their apex. The columns are then erected and the roof structure cables are tensioned to full strength. For the New York building the roof membrane was spread over paired rafter frames before craning this unit into position, however, for the others it is spread over the entire roof structure after it is complete. Fabric end walls are erected, and pitched fabric 'roof' sections placed in between the containers to make the building

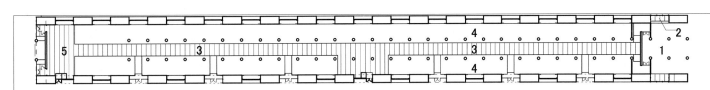

2

3

1 Nomadic Museum, New York, USA 2005.
2/3 Plan and interior view.

weather-tight. Interior fittings, lighting, and audio-visual equipment are then installed.

A wooden plank runway surrounded by river stones creates a central route to view Colbert's 200 photographs, which are suspended in front of the containers between the columns. The 4000 square metre building was in use for four months in New York before being dismantled – it then relocated to Santa Monica, Los Angeles, in January 2006. In 2007 it opened in Odaiba, Tokyo. For these later shows the building form was changed from a single continuous space to two side-by-side buildings with a simple fabric-roofed space added between the two main volumes. This monumental structure belies its mobile status in form; however, the existing 'used' character of the containers remains to remind visitors of the structure's main building block. Colbert's atmospheric pictures are perfectly suited to the powerful internal atmosphere accentuated by careful lighting and the audio-visual installation that punctuates the exhibition.

Tectoniks Ltd.
Spirit of Dubai Building

2007
Designers/Engineers: Tectoniks Ltd., Shropshire, UK;
Steve Casselman, David Kelsall, Rob Greene
Client: Nakheel LLC

Engineers David Kelsall and Steve Casselman are designers who have made a dramatic journey in their careers that is proof of the capacity for technology transfer to have a significant impact on design development in a different field. As design and production engineers for the Lindstrand Balloon company they were engaged in the manufacture of a series of innovative aircraft for commercial and record-breaking clients. These included balloons and airships in many different sizes, shapes, and designs. In 1999, Lindstrand was asked to build a membrane structure for the millennium celebrations in Sweden. The project was designed and built in just five weeks from stitched balloon fabric and medium-weight PVC-coated polyester fabric and erected in four days onto a scaffolding framework. The central section alone was 47.5 metres long, 18 metres wide and 11.5 metres high. Important lessons were learnt from this first building – stitched joints leaked air, requiring the structure to have huge blowers to keep it inflated, and the areas where balloon fabric was used, though lightweight, had insufficient strength. The success of this project led to a commission to create a second inflatable building structure with Lindstrand for the award-

winning Magna Science Adventure Centre in Yorkshire, UK, designed by Wilkinson Eyre Architects. The facility comprised three structures; an 18 metre diameter restaurant for 200 people, a 10 metre diameter children's play area, and a 32 metre long educational centre, all situated within the converted former steelworks. This was their first building structure to use industry-standard welded joints and architectural fabrics by Ferrari. Whilst at Lindstrand, Kelsall also designed his first mobile inflatable buildings including an 18 metre by 12 metre aircraft hangar that can be deployed within an hour with a 'clamshell' door that can be opened and closed in seconds.

In 2004, Kelsall, Casselman, and Greene formed their own company to focus specifically on inflatable buildings – in 2006 it became Tectoniks. Tectoniks design and manufacture a wide range of inflatable buildings, intended for both static and mobile situations. Their products are both specially commissioned and standard designs intended to provide generic solutions, however, the basic constructional philosophy remains the same. Tectoniks use Autocad as a basic software design tool but they have also written their own software for pattern generation, stress

1

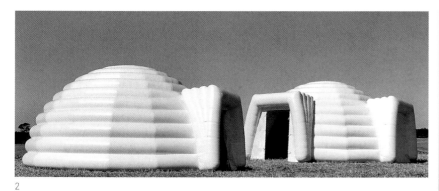

2

3

1 The Spirit of Dubai Building, Dubai,
United Arab Emirates.
2/3 Tectoniks commercial 7 metre
span dome and the Tectoniks installation
at the Magna Science Adventure Centre,
Yorkshire, UK.

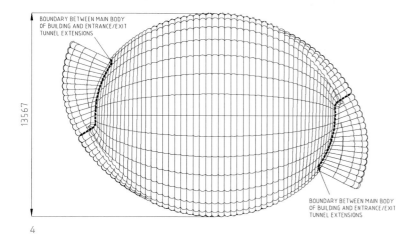

BOUNDARY BETWEEN MAIN BODY
OF BUILDING AND ENTRANCE/EXIT
TUNNEL EXTENSIONS

13567

BOUNDARY BETWEEN MAIN BODY
OF BUILDING AND ENTRANCE/EXIT
TUNNEL EXTENSIONS

4

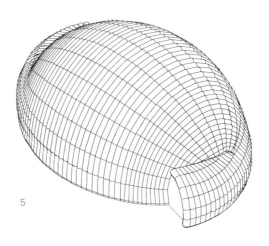

5

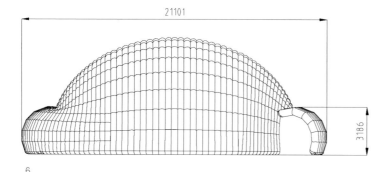

21101

3186

6

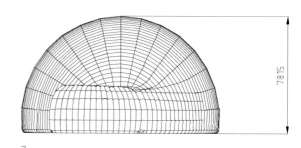

7815

7

analysis, and artwork manipulation. Two layers of fire-retardant PVC polyester fabric are combined into shapes that have a cavity filled with pressurised air. All joints are welded to enable the structure to operate at a comparatively high pressure. The internal air pressure of the structure is automatically monitored and activates the blowers to keep the structure taut – because of the high quality welding system the blowers only need to operate for a short amount of time. The buildings are restrained in soft ground by spiral steel anchors, and water ballast containers on hard ground. Standard designs include domes, clear span arches, and open-air structures that pivot to allow a clear view of the interior. The practical limit for the standard clear span structures is 25 to 30 metres because of cost, but it is technically possible to create a clear span structure of 60 metres using existing materials and methods. Clients do not always appreciate that these temporary structures are also reusable and if they have no further need for the building Tectoniks will sometimes buy them back for reuse for another purpose. All of the company's buildings are made in the Tectoniks factory using a CNC (computer numeric controlled) cutter and

specialised welders. Prototyping is rare because of cost, even for bespoke buildings, although they are modelled extensively on the computer for form and stress. Completed structures are tested in the factory for several days prior to delivery, with pressures of up to one and a half times operating levels. The Building Research Establishment is used for advanced testing. A 17.5 metre by 11 metre by 8.5 metre aircraft hangar can be erected in 30 minutes, a 7 metre span dome in 20 minutes. Weather conditions do not have to be perfect but it should not be excessively windy as the structures are vulnerable in their half-inflated state. Structures are transported in crates that can be moved by a standard forklift truck.

The most ambitious commissioned structure that Tectoniks has built so far is the Spirit of Dubai Terminal for the airship of the same name, which is the largest in the world. The building provided the arrival facility for the airship's journey through Europe in order to draw attention to the huge waterfront development in the United Arab Emirates, The Dubai Palm. The building was manufactured in the UK and then delivered to the site in Dubai in two crates, one for the membrane and one for

8

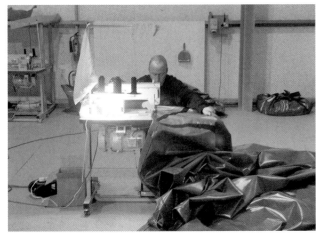

9

10

11

the pressurisation and other equipment. A base was prepared in advance and erection was completed in a single
day. The membrane was spread out on the base, the
blowers connected and in 40 minutes it was fully erected.
The building requires four small 375-watt (0.5 hp) blowers
connected to a programmable logic controller, which
continually monitors pressure. The blowers are connected
to the structure by 50 millimetre diameter hoses (which
can be buried underground if required). Only two operate
in normal conditions and they are virtually inaudible in the
building. The building was anchored to the ground using
resin anchors rated at 500 kilograms each. If the building is
relocated to soft ground, spiral anchors can be used that
have the same rating. If a puncture occurs the blowers keep
the building inflated, even in the case of a large rupture.
During the fitting-out process a forklift truck tore a large
hole in the fabric, however, a repair was soon made without
the need to take the building down.

12   13   14

4–7 Plan, isometric view, side and front
elevation.
8–11 Tectoniks manufacturing facility –
all buildings are built in the factory and trial
assembled prior to shipping. The partly
inflated Spirit of Dubai building bottom right.
12–14 Restraint webbing; air supply pump
and controls; air supply hose.

James Law Cybertecture

Pacific Century Cyberworks Connect Kiosk Shops

2004–2007
Architect: James Law Cybertecture, Hong Kong, China
Client: Pacific Century Cyberworks (PCCW)

Hong Kong-based architect James Law heads up a multi-disciplinary design team whose projects cross the boundaries between architecture, industrial design, product design, interiors, and IT. He describes his practice as 'cybertecture', working in a field that covers everything from one-to-one interaction to whole cityscapes. The environments he designs are intended to have a symbiotic balance between physical space and technology, between actual objects and computer-mediated situations. These 'places', which are often transient or changeable, utilise a mixture of user-operable and invisible technology to create more responsive architecture and interiors in order to improve efficiency for the operator and to heighten the visitor experience.

Law trained as an architect in the UK and worked in Tokyo with Itsuku Hasegawa and in the US with Gensler International prior to setting up his own practice in 2001. The principle behind 'cybertecture' is the ambition to give a space its own intelligence so that it can interact with its users. Law uses a wide range of electronic devices to create these 'aware' environments: infrared location, electronic tagging, fibre-optic projectors, and animatronics.

Immediately after it was established, Law's practice began work on the design of a new software-based artificial intelligence called S.I.G.N.A.L. that communicates directly with people via voice recognition, human presence detectors, and a controller interface. The Hong Kong government commissioned the development of the concept into a full-size interactive mock-up entitled the Artificial Intelligence Media Laboratory. Law created a physical environment in which the artificial intelligence cyber character controlled mechanical servos to move walls, a hydraulic floor table, audio-visual systems, and animatronics devices. The environment was not intended to be a static physical place into which these electronic systems were fixed, but a changing, flexible environment that was altered by the devices in response to the desires and needs of the user.

In 2004, Law was invited by IBM Europe and the Danish Tolvanen corporation to collaborate on a house design that challenged conventional forms of domestic space, and instead has the ability to move and reshape itself in response to the inhabitants' needs. The concept was to create a dwelling in which the physical space could be asresponsive and interactive as a personal computer

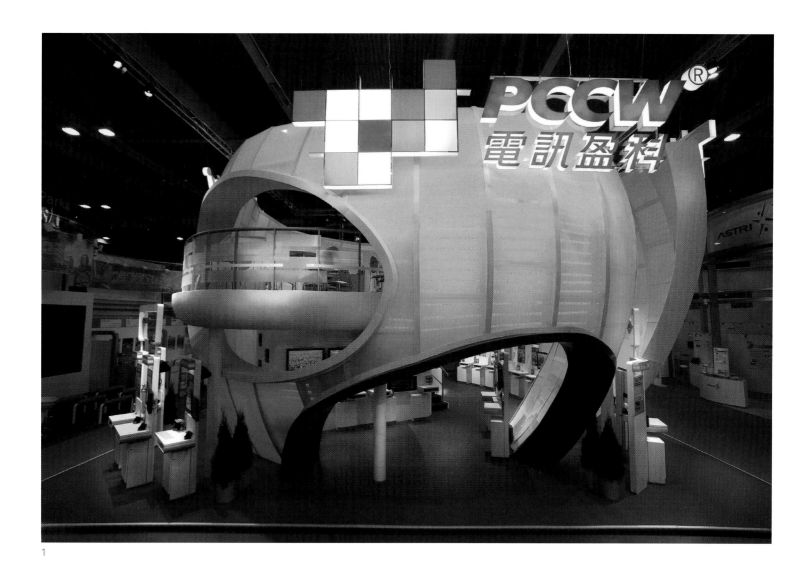

1

2

1/2 PCCW mobile showroom for use
in interior environments such as expos.

3

4

5

6

3–6 The PCCW system can be adapted
to a wide variety of installation situations,
here on permanent and temporary sites
in Hong Kong.
7–10 PCCW system components.
11 Proposed layout plan.

interface. The house consists of three zones of equal size –
two sets of rooms on two floors that stand on either side
of a central double-height atrium space. The house has its
own cyber character (a virtual butler), which residents
access via a voice recognition system. Sensors activate the
control system upon residents' presence in the various
parts of the house. The surrounding rooms are like drawers
that move in and out of the central space, changing both
the way it operates and its appearance.

Since 2002, James Law has designed a range of mobile
and flexible facilities for Hong Kong's largest telecom-
munications and IT company, Pacific Century Cyberworks
(PCCW). Although PCCW had a conventional presence in
fixed shops they wanted to create a new sort of environment for the company's customers that would make them
more accessible but would also expand their market presence in a flexible, responsive manner. This meant moving
away from conventional static shops to mobile locations
with direct access to existing and potential new customers.
The proposal was therefore to establish a linked chain
of shops, exhibition stands, mobile shops, and kiosks.
The shops are in permanent locations, although they are

still flexible in layout. The exhibition stands are created
to have an individual, arresting presence at shows but
still convey the company image. Mobile shops are intended
to provide the same retail experience to customers as
permanent facilities though they can move from place to
place. The kiosks are smaller, fast-relocating units that
can be set up in public places such as shopping malls.
An important part of the concept was that although the
various facilities were distributed to a wide variety of
locations, they would be interactively linked to the company's IT network – in theory creating a series of shop
counters, which no matter where they were physically
located, were still virtually in the company's 'shop'.

Law began with the development of a capsule that has
a recognisable general design theme in order to allow the
PCCW brand identity to be recognisable to the customer
between shop, exhibition stand, mobile shop, and kiosk.
The capsule is a mobile display trolley with pre-wired
power and communications connections allowing a wide
range of phone, PDA, desktop, and laptop products to be
displayed in active mode. Easily changeable logo and
advertising systems are also incorporated. An individual

7

8

9

10

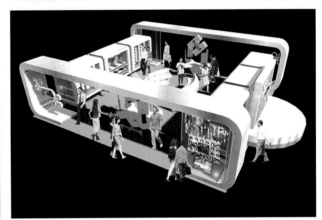

radio frequency identity (RF-id) tag acting in the same way as a computer's IP address enables the module to be tracked by location. A microprocessor logs each of the products on sale, including their price. The capsule is designed to transport the products safely, but when at the shop location it can be opened out to allow customers and sales staff access. The capsule is accompanied by portable counters, showcases, video display stands and, for the exhibition stands and mobile shops, portals as well as walls to mark the shop entrance and define its space. These also have RF-id tags that allow their location to be tracked. The capsules' construction is made from conventional shop-fitting materials, standard timber, metal, and composite parts, and they are prefabricated in the factory of a specialist shop fitter. All parts are designed for easy movement and transportation in a standard truck. Set up of the mobile kiosks takes from two to six hours depending on complexity.

11

LOT-EK

DIM Mobile Retail Unit
Uniqlo Pop-Up Store

The possibility of adapting materials and construction techniques from other industries into architecture has been frequently advocated since the beginning of the twentieth century and although many exciting prototypes exist, the full impact of widespread technology transfer has yet to be exploited. Portable architecture uses a much wider range of materials and constructional techniques than conventional building projects and it is therefore at the forefront in the exploitation of technology transfer opportunities in the building industry. However, it is not always innovative, cutting-edge technology that has proven the best resource.

The work of New York design firm LOT-EK is not only inspired by industrial products but frequently uses them in its construction. Italian architects Giuseppe Lignano and Ada Tolla have recognised not only the practicality but the beauty of the familiar facilities and machines that serve urban living: oil tankers, refrigerators, steel sinks, and shipping containers have all been used to make interiors and new buildings. LOT-EK create a surprisingly bespoke architectural vision by making new architecture from old objects. Their work nevertheless conveys a contemporary image that has connotations of recycling and mobility.

Simply using a large object originally manufactured for another purpose means that mobility becomes an issue, if only to move it from the place in which it has been found to the place in which it is to be converted. However, mobility is also an intrinsic component in their overall design agenda – particularly in the projects that have involved shipping containers. The shipping container is a tough, modular, movable tool that is incorporated into a worldwide standard for ease of transportation. It is obvious that a building form based on this module can make use of the readily available cranes, lorries, and ships for relocation purposes and it is common practice to convert shipping containers to make simple, temporary, secure storage facilities, site-huts, and rudimentary offices etc.

LOT-EK's first realised mobile shipping container project was the Welcome Box for the Liverpool Biennial of Contemporary Art in 2002, though they had proposed many other projects before that including a mobile restaurant, American Diner #1 (1996), and an entry for the design competition for a Slave Trade Memorial at Dakar, Senegal

1   DIM Mobile Retail Unit
in transportation mode.

(1997). Sited to greet arriving visitors on the London platform at the city's railway station, the Welcome Box pre-
sented a familiar object that had also clearly been morphed
into something quite different that was both an art installation and a building with a practical use. Ramped entrances
at each end led into a mirrored and black rubber-padded
interior in which video monitors projected changing images
with an accompanying soundtrack. Manufactured in a local
workshop and delivered to site and commissioned within
24 hours, the building was removed after three months and
placed in storage to wait for the next event.

Though created within an existing building structure,
the Bohen Contemporary Art Foundation, New York, (2003)
utilised containers as movable 'rooms' set around the
periphery of a contemporary art space in the meat-packing
district. The skins of the containers were cut and bent to
form windows, doorways, and even furniture. Set on wheels
they can be relocated easily simply by pushing them along
a track. They form part of a flexibility strategy for the
gallery, which also includes large mobile walls suspended
on tracks.

DIM Mobile Retail Unit

2005
Architect: LOT-EK, Giuseppe Lignano and Ada Tolla,
New York, USA
Interaction Designer: Inbar Barak, New York, USA
Client: Sara Lee Corporation

The French DIM label makes fashionable clothing focusing
on underwear, lingerie, and hosiery with a target audience
aged 20 to 35. The concept for the Mobile Retail Unit was
for a shop that travelled to wherever the shopper would be.
People could log on to the DIM website to find out where
the store was at that time, typically outside concert venues,
universities, or existing shopping malls – places where
the chance of passing trade were also high. LOT-EK worked
in collaboration with IT designer Inbar Barak to make a
highly interactive facility that shoppers could engage with
not only to 'arrange' a meeting place but also in terms of
physically operating aspects of its interior. The shop was
built in 2004 by North Carolina-based truck and coach

2

builders Spevco, on a standard 16 metre long, 90 square metre truck frame, which triples in size by opening full-length push-out elements that are mechanically operated. Computer controlled hydraulic pistons operate the extending elements which are strong enough to support the cantilever, however, adjustable legs drop down for added security. Full-length windows in the shape of the company brand name allow views of the illuminated interior, and sealing at the joints of the fixed and push-out elements is by a rubber gasket. These pull-out elements dictate the position of the fixed elements such as clothing stacks and accessory drawers, which are positioned down the centre of the truck. The relatively lightweight fitting rooms and lounge seats are positioned in the extending sections.

The DIM clothing range is updated rapidly, typically once every two weeks. Vertical pull-out drawers contain the clothes and each has a video camera inside and a series of flat video screens on the front. Shoppers can see what is in the drawers and as they pull out the item their hands are also displayed on the screen. People can also take a digital snapshot of their face when they open the drawers, which is then displayed on the highest level monitors creating

an ever-changing community montage. The video screens also display advertising images of the clothes that are contained in the drawers. Power can be provided independently from the on-board generator in the truck's tractor unit, however, for longer-term situations the facility can also be plugged into an external generator or mains supply. The shoppers operate the fitting spaces too, which drop down concertina-like from the ceiling to save space when not in use, but also to create a changing, dynamic interior feature. There are no fixed tills; a mobile, restaurant-style hand-held machine is taken to the shopper when they have decided on their purchase. The reflective interior surfaces enhance the constantly shifting video display.

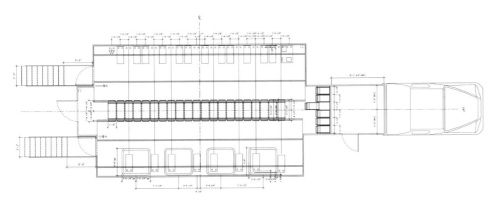

PLAN

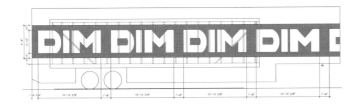

SIDE ELEVATION

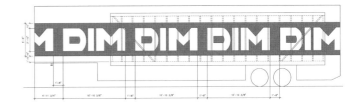

SIDE ELEVATION

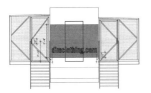

REAR ELEVATION

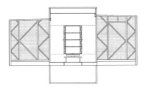

FRONT ELEVATION

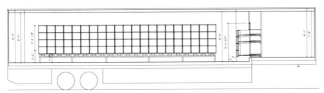

LOGITUDINAL SECTION

LONGITUDINAL SECTION

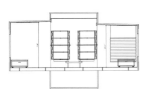

CROSS SECTION

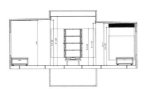

CROSS SECTION

2 DIM Mobile Retail Unit in operational mode.
3 Plans, sections, and elevations in operational mode.

4/5 DIM Mobile Retail Unit interior
showing the video fronted drawers.

1

1 Uniqlo Pop-Up Store on site in Manhattan,
New York, USA.

Uniqlo Pop-Up Store

2006
Architect: LOT-EK, Giuseppe Lignano and Ada Tolla,
New York, USA
Client: Uniqlo

Another mobile shop facility designed by LOT-EK is the
Uniqlo Pop-Up Store, created for the Japanese firm whose
philosophy is based on high-quality products with a
minimal aesthetic sold at affordable prices. Uniqlo has
many fixed outlets in Japan and Europe that sell its comparatively limited range of well-designed, simple clothes,
stationery, furniture, and household objects. LOT-EK
designed the company's flagship store in Osaka, Japan,
called Uniqlo+, which included a container element that
protruded from the main elevation to hold the main shop
sign. In order to introduce the company to the US market
it commissioned two mobile shops that could be situated
temporarily at prominent sites, beginning in New York
City in 2006. LOT-EK's expertise in the reapplication
of container technology to provide surprising modern

environments fitted well with Uniqlo's philosophy of
minimal yet functional contemporary design. The shops
were fitted into a 6 metre long, 16 square metre standard
ISO container with the minimum of structural alterations
so it could retain its strength. Openings are restricted
to one side of the container; a doorway is split horizontally,
opening up to provide an entrance ramp and a canopy;
and five vertical floor to ceiling windows provide glimpses
of the illuminated interior. A simple clothes rack lines the
opposite wall, with smaller pull-down fitting spaces based
on the same concept as the DIM store, and a cash wrap,
and till area. The shop is transported on a standard
'knuckle-boom' truck that has its own crane for loading
and off-loading. The shop can be delivered to any urban
roadside location and be in use in minutes, plugging into
external infrastructure for power.

   LOT-EK's work clearly responds to a particular aesthetic that is robust and functional. It draws on familiar
industrial products and reinvents them into a contemporary architecture that has a coherent image. Their designs
do not rely on technological innovation for inspiration or
construction but on tried and trusted systems utilised in

2

novel ways. LOT-EK communicate ideas about their work by extremely clear and pragmatic images and words, refusing to be drawn into theoretical discussions about their sources. This architecture exhibits its capability for movement in its resilience and toughness rather than in a lightweight aesthetic. It could be argued that it is a definitively urban mobile architecture, making use of familiar elements such as trucks and containers that merge into the city landscape seamlessly. Though their projects invariably find new roles for these objects they bring along their existing character with them, indeed LOT-EK are concerned to reinforce the containers' history utilising raw materials in their conversion, such as steel, aluminium, and plywood, as well as primary colours and large-scale letter graphics. An important factor in the success of LOT-EK's mobile architecture is that it does not erase the essence of mobility of the products from which it is made, but uses this to reinforce its character.

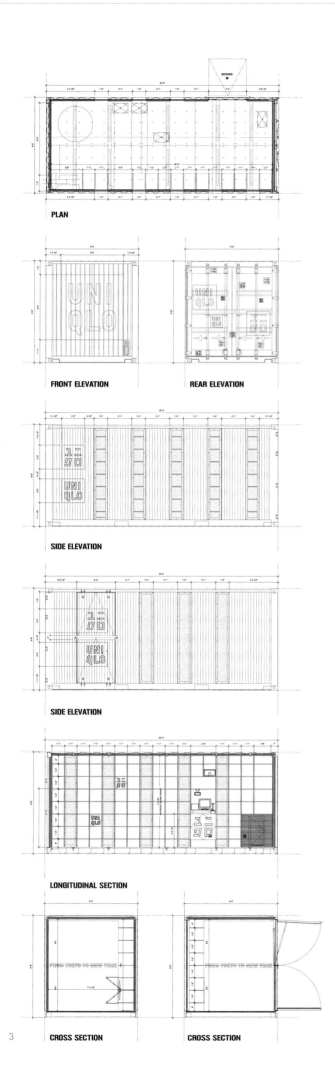

PLAN

FRONT ELEVATION   **REAR ELEVATION**

SIDE ELEVATION

SIDE ELEVATION

LONGITUDINAL SECTION

3   **CROSS SECTION**   **CROSS SECTION**

4

5

2 The Uniqlo permanent store in Japan –
a container is used as an identifying emblem
that connects it to the mobile units.
3 Uniqlo plans, sections, and elevations.
4/5 Deployment process using standard
container forklift truck and road container
delivery vehicle.

Inflate
Big M
Unipart Structure
Smirnoff Cube

Product design has an established history of objects that have been designed and constructed within the same organisation for delivery in completed form, ready for operation. In vehicle design there are many examples of cars, service vehicles, aircraft, ships, and trains that have become classic examples of a fine-tuned response to a specific problem. The idea of building as product design has been explored, but hardly ever fully implemented. The method of making buildings by using the process of coordinated, factory-based manufacture has dramatic advantages in terms of construction speed and efficiency, however, as in product manufacture it is very important that design remains tuned to user and client requirements so that quality is not eroded.

Nick Crosbie, founder of the design innovation company Inflate, first started working with pneumatic structures whilst at Central Saint Martin's College in London in the early 1990s, where his final degree show project was for an inflatable, floating television. Crosbie believes that plastic is a material that required a new language from its inception but this was misunderstood and instead it was used to replicate other materials – indeed the use of plastic became almost synonymous with the belief that a product made from it was inexpensive. Crosbie also perceived plastic as a naturally colourful material, which because it was cheap, was open to study for new uses. He found it could be assembled quickly and easily using high-frequency welding in a process that is comparable to sewing fabric. Rather than designing products on paper and then creating the object to look like the design, Crosbie discovered that experimentation with the material was the best route to discovering what it could do – exploration, invention, and happy mistakes led to Inflate's first successful products. These are beautifully made but still mass-market household objects – a fruit-bowl, a picture-frame, a wine-rack. These products are also witty and fun – an eggcup shaped like a life preserver being a typical example. Even though the material is cheap, Inflate's domestic products are beautifully made and carefully designed in detail so that they are as efficient to produce as possible.

Crosbie also set out to create a brand that was perceived as quality-design led. Crucial to Inflate's developing presence was the annual 100% Design show in London at which the company has exhibited since its inception.

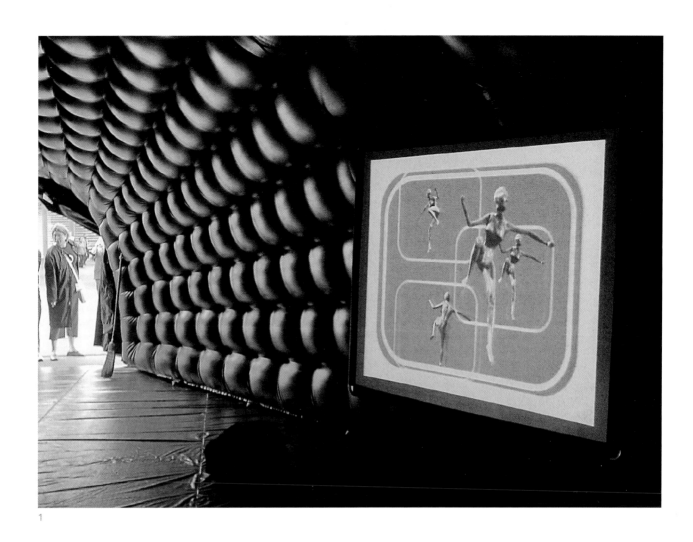

1   Big M exhibition structure interior.

Exhibitions like this result in companies having to think
carefully about the spaces in which they show their
products and for Inflate this led to their first environmen-
tal-scale designs that were big enough for people to enter.
The move of 100% Design to a much larger, but lower
quality, exhibition arena in 1998 induced Crosbie to create
a controlled environment made from an air-supported
cube which visitors had to be zipped in and out of – a
novelty that added to its success.

2

2 View from above showing the three
principal inflated elements.

Big M

2000
Designer: Inflate, London, UK
Consultants: Tom Cullen (Technical Designer),
Simon Northrop (Project Concept), Michelle Hirschom
(Exhibition Curator)
Client: ISIS Arts

Designing larger structures is different from designing
mass-market products in that they can usually be considered one-off objects. The 'Big M' was a commission to
create a mobile exhibition structure that could travel
around in a van with three people who would both set it up
and man it. The client was ISIS Arts, a Northeast England-
based, not-for-profit arts organisation that promotes and
develops art projects. They wanted a mobile venue that
could be used to communicate video and digital media to
a wide range of people. Crosbie was interested in applying
simple construction technology to make more sophisticated structures. The portable and inflatable play structures typically called 'bouncy castles' are a big market,

with many small-scale manufacturers operating in the
UK and elsewhere. With such competition, production is
driven very much by low-cost pricing and so quality is generally not high. Crosbie decided nevertheless to develop
this technology for use with the 'Big M'. The building was
designed using small-scale models to develop a form that
used a number of identical panels for economy, which when
laced together made an unusual but stable form because
of the compound shape of the three elements. The building
is 17 metres across at its widest point and 5 metres high
and is made from polyester reinforced PVC. In the darkened
interior a touch-screen interface allows visitors to choose
their own video show on three screens with simultaneous
stereo sound. Despite its simple construction the structure
is strong enough to support people on its roof and is robust
enough to have been used on widely varying sites around
the UK for seven years.

1

1 Unipart exhibition structure exterior view.

Unipart Structure

2005
Designer: Inflate, London, UK
Engineer: Webb Yates, London, UK
Client: With and Unipart

In 2005, Inflate was commissioned to design a mobile exhibition structure for communications agency With for their client Unipart. A large-scale manufacturer of automotive components, Unipart sponsored the annual Goodwood Festival of Speed, which is the largest historic motor-racing event to take place in the UK. With asked Inflate to design a building that conveyed the impression of a contemporary museum. The resulting structure is 8 metres high and 350 square metres on plan. It is once more a hybrid structure, but this time with a much simpler and more elegant metal support – a single elliptical arch onto which two inflatable panels are mounted. The only other 'hard' elements are the doorframes at each end. The inflated panels therefore fulfil a much more important structural role – and they also gen-

erate a sinuous, streamlined, symmetrical truncated cone form. Internally, the building is used as a mobile museum displaying the history and current operations of the Unipart company, with four gallery environments containing vehicles, sculptures, and products. The building was manufactured by Envelope Structures Ltd., a company set up by Crosbie to handle the production side of Inflate's output.

2

3

2/3   Interior view of the Unipart showing
the internal metal arch. Exterior showing the
mirror image inflatable tubes.

1

1 Computer rendered drawing of the
Smirnoff Cube.

Smirnoff Cube

2006
Designer: Inflate, London, UK
Engineer: Webb Yates, London, UK
Client: Itch and Smirnoff

Envelope also made Inflate's most ambitious mobile
building to date, the Cube, a mobile nightclub commissioned by event marketing agency Itch for its client
Smirnoff. It is not in itself very large but has a complex
form not usually associated with inflatable structures.
The Smirnoff brand aims at being 'cool' and fun – and
the requirement for this building was to create an image
that conveyed this. The building form is therefore reminiscent of a floating 15 metre square ice-cube suspended
above the ground. The 180 square metre structure is
erected entirely from ground level and it can accommodate
300 people at one time. The aluminium framing is assembled first and then the inflatable cube is assembled on
this – the white reinforced PVC cube self-erects as it is
inflated. Interlocking Rola Trac Snap lock plastic decking

is set up inside and an inflatable DJ's booth sits in one
corner. Platipus ground anchors are fixed into the ground
at key points with smaller Spira Locks used elsewhere.
The aluminium trusses are designed to support lighting
and music equipment as well as the inflated building skin.
The entire building packs into four packages each less
than a metre cube and weighing 530 kilogrammes in total.
It takes a day to set up with a crew of twelve and four
small cherry-picker vehicles. The power source to keep
the structure inflated is five 0.75 hp fans, which operate
off a normal 220 to 240 volt power supply or a generator.
A mobile proprietary 'Justincase' drinks bar system is used
for flexibility. The building is typically used at open-air
festival events such as the Isle of Wight 2006 event where
it made its debut.

Innovation in Inflate's work comes not from the application of advanced technology but from the inventive use
of relatively simple, affordable, easily available materials
and construction methods. Product development is still
a big inspiration, carried out at a large scale through the
manufacturing company Envelope but also increasingly
through the company's Hong Kong office and its new,

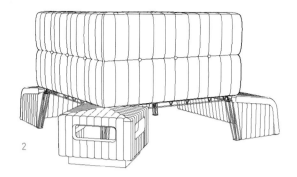

2

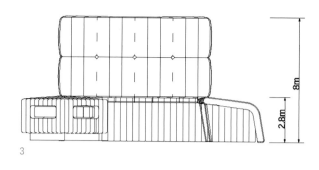

3

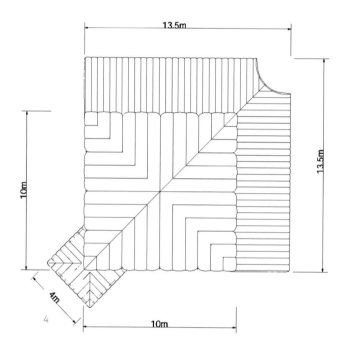

4

dedicated factory in China. Inflate offers a complete service
to clients from concept to design to manufacture to operation of the building on site, however, many are owned and
operated by the clients themselves or by specialist rigging
and staging companies such as Gallowglass. The pneumatic components provide many benefits such as quick
assembly, easy erection, cheap manufacture and being
waterproof, insulative, and easy to repair and replace (the
buildings come with their own quick repair kits). Cutting
patterns are developed primarily using Rhino software
though Form-Z is also used sometimes. Strength of materials and jointing is an integral problem in the design of
pneumatic structures – by using hybrid methods to build
larger buildings, Inflate bypasses this problem. The building
designs are not 'pure' in the sense that they are totally
honest in appearance – the Unipart building appears from
the outside to be a completely air-supported structure
when in fact it is a hybrid. However, this hardly matters
because the pneumatic cladding is so light that the
supporting aluminium frames can also be light. In fact this
lack of purity is part of their charm – like Inflate's household products, its buildings seem fun and mischievous.

5

6

2–4 Perspective, front elevation, and plan.
5/6 Smirnoff Cube exterior publicity image
and interior view of the assembled structure
– a mixture of bespoke components and
standard bar and furnishing systems.

Festo

Airtecture Air Hall

Airquarium

Festo is a world leading manufacturer in the field of pneumatics and their actuator, sensor, and processor products are used in virtually all industries where automation is a feature of the manufacturing process. This is a high-tech business that encompasses every aspect of the world's industrial output from motor manufacturing to milk production. Festo maintains a presence in more than 170 countries and has 56 subsidiary companies. The company has a vision of the future in which innovation is the key to success, and since the early 1990s it has developed a range of innovative, cutting edge prototype products that not only break new ground in terms of technology but also play a part in developing the public image of the company. These design engineering products are based around the company's core expertise of pneumatics, however, the range of applications goes far beyond their normal production engineering expertise and includes aviation innovations in ballooning and powered aircraft. The philosophy can best be described by Festo's motto 'Air in Air' which encapsulates the idea that the air itself can be a powerful force in the generation and operation of machines and structures.

Airtecture Air Hall

1996–2000
Designer/Engineer: Festo Corporate Design,
Esslingen, Germany
Client: Festo KG

The term 'Airtecture' does not refer to a single building but the philosophy of making conventional building elements such as columns, walls, roofs, or windows from membranes prestressed with air. With the use of sensors, actuators, and computers they can have an interactive relationship with their environment, actively responding to input from weather monitoring equipment, which measures external wind loads, snow loads, and temperature changes. The use of air as a main constructional element makes the buildings lightweight, dynamic, and capable of achieving the highest levels of thermal insulation and energy efficiency. Developed under architecture-trained design engineer Axel Thallemer, the 'Airtecture' exhibition hall is the first building to incorporate this comprehensive approach throughout its construction and operational

1

systems. It has also been designed to be completely portable and can be packaged into a single standard ISO shipping container.

For the Airtecture Air Hall to be the exemplar of innovation that Festo desired, it was important that the final design should essentially be one without direct precedent. However, bionics was an influence on the original concept, the form of the distinctive 'Y'-shaped column in particular being derived from the shape of the wing of a dragonfly. Conventional inflatables were not an influence as Thallemer believed that these are comparatively simple, passive structures, whose form is only loosely determined by the structural system. Nevertheless, the Fuji Pavilion designed by Yutaka Murata for Expo 70 was influential because it consisted solely of interconnected high-pressure air beams formed into an organic tunnel-like shape over a circular plan. At the time it was built it stretched the current technology both in membrane design and in pneumatic control systems to the limit.

The Airtecture Air Hall encloses a rectangular 375 square metre internal space that is 6 metres high. This volume has the flat walls and flat ceilings of conventional building forms and therefore is quite different from most tensile membrane buildings which must usually consist of the double curved surfaces that form the strongest pneumatic structural system. The outside of the hall is quite different to the interior and can best be described as an exoskeleton. This supporting structure consists of 40 6 metre high 'Y'-shaped columns, linked together by 12.7 metre long horizontal air beams and braced by vertical and diagonal pneumatic muscles. The columns and air beams are made of a conventional synthetic fabric, polyamide, and coated with a Hypalon flame-inhibiting elastomer coating.

The air beams range in diameter from 0.75 metres at the ends to 1.25 metres at mid-span and are fixed with stainless steel connectors to the walls and column points and located laterally over their span by textile belts. Stainless steel cables and struts are also used where remote element-to-element connections are required. When viewed in plan the top points of the 'Y'-shaped columns rotate back and forth to triangulate the structure. The building's longitudinal stability is aided by two sets of diagonal pneumatic muscles at either end of the building. These are also used at every column bay to stabilise the

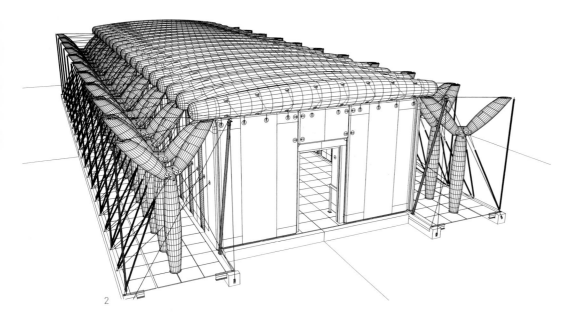

2

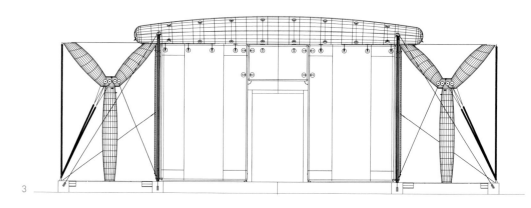

3

building across its width. The muscles are made of polyamide fabric with an internal silicone hose. Unlike a conventional tensile cable, which is tensioned only once when a building is completed, this element is constantly regulated by varying the internal air pressure between 0.3 and 1 bar providing a wide variation in axial force. The air beams can be pretensioned in the same way to resist variable wind and snow loads.

The walls consist of specially developed, double-skin, air-tensioned polyamide membrane 'slabs'. These wall units are 200 millimetres thick, the two surface membranes continuously coupled by 72,000 threads per square metre and tensioned by air pressure at 0.5 bar. This system has been developed from carpet weaving tufting technol-ogy in order to make a flat 'wall' element from tensile membrane components, which normally require curved surfaces to attain their rigidity and stability. Natural light is admitted through Velaglas membrane envelopes, a new chemically altered natural rubber that takes the form of a transparent elastomer. In the roof these envelopes maintain rigidity through a partial vacuum. The structural stability of the roof is therefore achieved by alternating

structural elements using positive and negative air pressure. These 'window' areas also provide the tolerance for movement throughout the entire structure.

The building has more than 330 individual air-supported elements with varying air pressures and volumes. For control purposes these elements are grouped into ten identical sections. The air pressure levels are controlled by proportional valves and the real-time pressure within the elements is monitored by sensors, which automatically release excess pressure through relief valves. A single computer controls a subset of ten slave computers, varying the pressure in individual elements according to climatic conditions. The building was designed to resist a 180 kilometres per hour wind speed combined with a simultaneous snow load of 80 kilogrammes per square metre. The highest wind yet experienced has been 220 kilometres per hour and the building did not move at all, though the extra air pressure in the structural elements meant that it swelled by 600 millimetres overall. During this extreme wind the designers further tested the building's systems by instructing the computer to loosen one third of all the pneumatic muscles thereby simulating

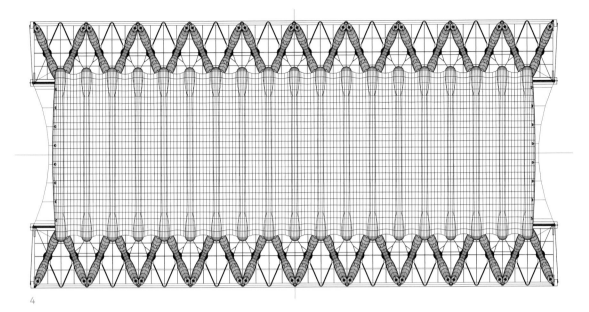

4

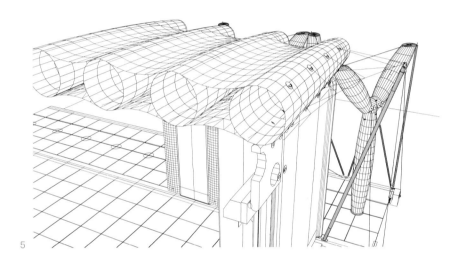

2/3 Airtecture Air Hall, computer
generated perspective and section.
4 Roof plan.
5 Perspective section through air beams.

5

a wind load of 250 kilometres per hour. The result was
the walls shivered! However, no damage was done.

This prototype 'Airtecture' hall was erected at the
Festo company headquarters in Esslingen, near Stuttgart,
Germany. Though designed as a mobile building, this
one sits on a steel frame system with a transparent metal
grid floor that allows the unique air pressure valve and
controls systems to be viewed in operation. Because this
was a new form of construction, communication between
the prototype manufacturer and the designers had to
be both instant and fluid. The building was designed
completely on computer and the specifications and drawings communicated to the manufacturing contractors
by the transmission of data files. The first air column fabric
joints were made in conventional membrane construction
manner with a lap joint, however, due to the extreme air
pressures demanded for this building these failed due
to excessive shear. A new pattern using butt joints with
an extra layer on each side was adopted which proved
successful. Once construction began no further changes
were made as the design had then been through an
extensive computer-based detail design period lasting

more than a year. Erection of the air-supported elements
took four days.

The main membrane manufacturer was the rubber
company Continental. Erection was undertaken by KOIT,
a company experienced in membrane construction. The
building was built for 8% under the original budget with all
costs and progress continuously monitored in the same
way as an industrial manufacturing project is controlled
using computer-based prediction systems. Construction
contracts were similar to those used for the development
of industrial manufacturing components.

Like many successful portable buildings, its deployment has become semi-permanent. Used as an exhibition,
seminar, and meeting hall, the benefits of having a con-
venient physical example of the company's most innovative product based permanently at their headquarters
is a valuable, easily utilised public relations tool. However,
the original intention of a portable exhibition building
that can communicate the company's skills throughout
the world is a valuable concept and a second Airtecture
Air Hall was completed and first exhibited at Expo 2000
in Hanover, Germany.

6

7

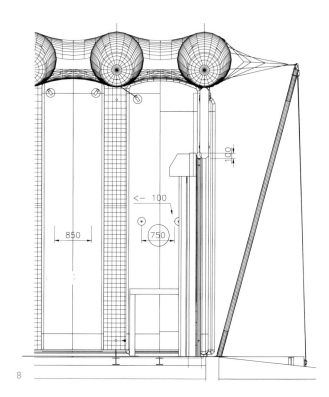

6/7 Side view showing the 'Y' columns, cable
bracing, and pneumatic muscles and
Airtecture Air Hall interior.
8 Section through top corner of the
end elevation showing the roof beams and
flat panel end walls.

8

This is the first attempt to make a building that is entirely self-monitored and self-controlled, its systems actuated automatically by computers and sensors. The objective was to create an intelligent, dynamic architecture. An appropriate simile might be the comparison of a 'fly-by-wire' aircraft to a conventional machine controlled by hand through physically activated controls. The computer control system in a modern cockpit not only enables the aircraft to outperform conventional designs, it also makes possible dramatic innovations in airframe and power systems design.

The robust character of the external structure is an important part of the building's image – it has been described as a cross between a Gothic cathedral and a pumped-up muscle man. Inside, the building hisses and clicks as the pressure valves open and shut in response to the commands of the computer. Though the continuous translucent panels that flow right around the building from wall to ceiling to wall are a relatively unusual feature, the overall interior space is formal and simple and there-fore appropriate for an exhibition hall interior which should not have an architecture that distracts from the display.

A computer terminal provides information about the temperature, air pressure, and condition of every element of the structure and internal environment – the building's condition can be monitored anywhere in the world via the internet. Calculations have suggested that if the control system were to be turned off completely it would be more than a week before the building began to sag ... just a little. The generous redundancy factor could be criticised for requiring constant energy to remain operable. However, its responsive nature indicates that this project is just the beginning of a development route that will eventually lead to buildings that are designed to exactly match their loading criteria rather than as now, to resist the worst possible conditions that may only ever happen once in their lifetime. Buildings that can respond actively to structural conditions in the same way that they already respond to temperature conditions – by the input of energy when it is needed – may result in a dramatic reduction in the material mass required to make them.

1 Airquarium in use as an exhibition
hall for 'Fifty Years of Italian and German
Design' in Bonn, Germany, 2000.

Airquarium

2000
Designer/Engineer: Festo Corporate Design,
Esslingen, Germany
Client: Festo KG

The Airquarium is the largest portable building designed
by Festo. It is a 32 metre diameter, air-supported dome
intended for use as an exhibition and event space. Lightweight membrane buildings that consist of a skin supported by a higher internal air pressure are not new – many
enormous structures exist including permanent roofs that
span huge sports stadia. However, Festo have taken a typically innovative approach to this building type pushing
back its performance capabilities in a number of areas.
It utilises a new Vitroflex membrane, which is unique in
several ways. It is remarkably translucent (it could even be
described as transparent) for such a large air-supported
structure – combining structural strength with a high
degree of connection to the world outside the dome was a
key aim of the Festo design team. In addition, this synthetic

material has been refined so that in case of fire only a
non-toxic vapour of water and vinegar would be released.
The building consists of a hemispherical dome that
is 9 metres high, restrained at the base by a tubular torus
that is filled with water to form a stable foundation.
The main air locked entrance cuts through the torus and is
big enough to admit large vehicles – there is a secondary
entrance that crosses over the torus for pedestrians.
A physical advantage of 'soft' air membrane construction
is that because of its flexibility it yields when subjected to
impact damage, and once the energy source is removed,
the structure is demountable for storage or redeployment.
The entire structure is carried in two 6 metre standard
containers. One holds the modular maintenance units for
air conditioning and ventilation, a water exchanger for
heating and cooling, a weather station with thermostatic
control and wind-load dependant air pressure control and
emergency generators that allow the building to operate
completely independently for up to 48 hours. The other
container transports the dome, the airlock, and the foundation membrane. The building can be installed on any solid
ground surface and takes six people a week to erect,

2

3

though much of this time is taken with filling up the torus with water. Airquarium is used as an exhibition hall and event and function space and has travelled to many venues since its construction.

In total, Festo has so far created 18 experimental pneumatic and membrane structures, though not all the building designs are mobile. The most recent is the Funnbrella, the world's largest single stem membrane shelter with a span of 31.6 metres and covered area of 998 square metres. The title is taken from the words 'funnel' and 'umbrella', however, its form was once again inspired by nature in the shape of the chanterelle mushroom. The structure can withstand a full load of snow resting asymmetrically on half of the umbrella surface – and near-hurricane strength winds.

Festo's building structures have been widely reported in industrial design and technical journals. The Airtecture Air Hall has won many industrial design awards including the Industrial Design Excellence Gold Award, the most prestigious US prize of this type. Despite this, it is surprising that they have had so little impact in the mainstream architectural press. Is this because they are so obviously

experimental designs? An outcome of blue-sky research and development rather than the ultimate solution to a widely recognised pragmatic problem? This is an important issue – if building contractors and component manufacturers do not take note of innovation, who will take the experimental results and apply them to the needs of the industry? Innovative technology cannot pass into use without general adoption by the building industry. The architectural profession needs to be aware of such developments and able to recognise their value and relevance to the live projects to which they are asked to find solutions. Architects have long argued that each and every design project is, in a way, a form of research and development, however, if the work they do is not breaking new ground or supplying new information this assertion is hard to justify. Genuine innovative research is risky, both in terms of the success or failure of the project objectives and in terms of money expended for an unquantifiable return, particularly if the results do not find a viable market. Festo's return on its 'Air in Air' proposals is as yet only quantifiable in terms of the company's improved image and increased publicity within the confines of their

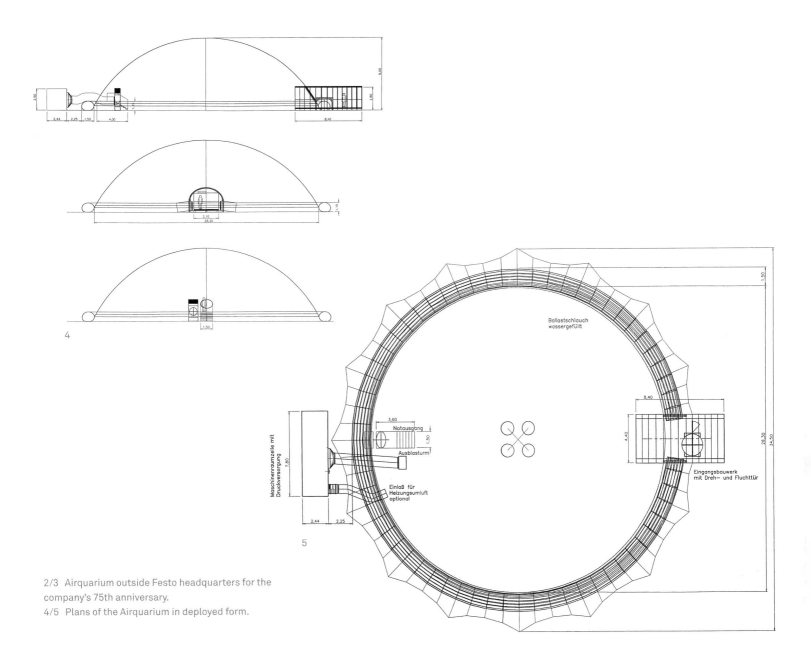

4

5

2/3 Airquarium outside Festo headquarters for the
company's 75th anniversary.
4/5 Plans of the Airquarium in deployed form.

manufacturing industry market, though its potential for
use in live projects in the greater scenario of world
construction has drawn interest from other designers.
Much has been said about the possible benefits to
architectural design of transfer technology from other
industries – here are examples that contain several new
technologies – pneumatic muscles, a transparent elastomer membrane, a woven three-dimensional double
wall structure, transparent non-flammable membranes.
In addition, these innovations are present in built working
examples that are clearly workable in practical terms
but also manage to communicate a provocative and exciting architectural form.

FTL Design Engineering Studio

Dyson Mobile Exhibition Pavilion

2004
Architect/Engineer: FTL Design Engineering Studio,
New York, USA
Client: EventQuest

FTL was founded in 1977 by Todd Dalland, joined by Nicholas Goldsmith in 1978, with the ambition to explore architecture as a technologically driven discipline. Goldsmith worked at Atelier Frei Otto in Stuttgart, Germany, between 1975 and 1977 and learnt Otto's development process for tensile structures that utilised physical modelling as a design tool and form generator. Physical modelling remains an important part of their design process, however, the firm has also adopted computer-modelling techniques for the dramatic improvements they offer in the design of complex structural forms.

FTL Design Engineering Studio has now worked on more than 800 separate projects and has won more than 30 awards for building work that has varied dramatically in size and function. Not all their work is tension structure-based, though even the prestigious interior design work for the big fashion houses of New York like Donna Karan and Calvin Klein began with the creation of temporary showrooms. The practice has designed and built many dramatic, permanent buildings. The Pier Six Concert Pavilion is located on Baltimore's Waterfront, and comprises a 3,500 seat concert pavilion with masonry stage

facilities and a 2,800 square metre tensile fabric roof structure. The Boston Harbor Lights Pavilion is a seasonal amphitheatre on Boston's Fan Pier. This building has seating for 4,500 people and its tensile roof covers an area of 3,700 square metres.

The lightweight nature of tensile structures means that they are particularly suitable for use in portable buildings and this has led to this type of building becoming an important part of FTL's workload. Todd Dalland has created designs for standard commercial marquee tents made by Anchor Industries Incorporated and Eureka Party Tents. Though these designs conform to standard layout patterns, their curved organic roof profiles still exhibit an elegant dynamic form. The tents use vinyl-laminated polyester fabric in modular patterns that incorporate repetitive erection and fixing components. A roof pattern may be repeated to form an unlimited size floor plan, though divided by vertical columns. Walls are separate from the roof structure and a number of different specifications are available including opaque, clear, mesh, and window patterns. Tent poles are obtainable in different materials and sizes that accommodate a variety of ground

1 Dyson Mobile Exhibition Pavilion
deployed at Lincoln Plaza, New York,
USA, 2004.

2

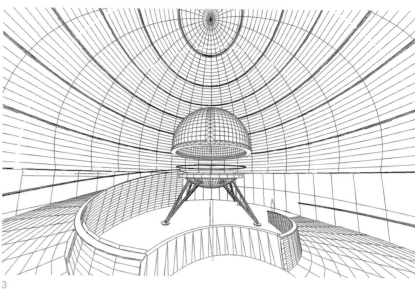

3

2 Deployment process – the membrane
is suspended from a crane as it is inflated.
3 Computer generated sketch design
model showing the interior.
4 Completed building interior.
5 Plan and sketch of ramp detail.

conditions and also allow a tent to be erected on an
uneven surface. An adjustable centre pole with a hand-
operated jack allows centre sections to be elevated with
ease to create dramatic internal spaces not possible
with conventional commercial marquees. However, it is
the specialised dedicated designs that are of greatest
interest in FTL's work.

In 2004, FTL Design Engineering Studio were commissioned by event management company EventQuest to
design a mobile structure that would promote Dyson products in North America. Dyson make high-quality, design-
led domestic appliances under the close direction of company founder James Dyson. The company's products are
technologically innovative but also have a very distinctive
image of uncompromising contemporary design using
bold colours. FTL's concept was to create a similarly bold,
colourful design at building scale that differed from
their usual mast supported tensile membrane expertise.
For this commercial project they proposed the idea of a
low-pressure air-supported dome based on a rigid framework containing the main exhibition area. In this way,
a high-quality exhibition of the company's products could

become the focus of the pavilion, with the environmental
shelter a comparatively simple yet bold contrasting
element that attracted public interest because of its
unusual external form.

The base structure is a tetrahedron steel pipe framework that encloses the water ballast foundations contained
in custom-made fabric sacks, and all the plant required
to inflate and power the structure. The base section has
double sidewalls with double doors set on each layer to
form the air lock to ensure the dome remains fully inflated
during use. A black internal sidewall contrasts with the
inflatable PVC polyester (Shelter-rite) yellow-coloured
dome that also doubles as a projection screen. Inside,
a separate structure contains the lighting and projection
rigs and a ramped walkway with an exhibition wall leading
to a smaller dome that contains an audio-visual display.
The building utilises a mixture of standard staging items
and specially made elements of which the 25 metre diameter dome is the largest. This is fixed at the perimeter
and suspended from the centre by a crane during inflation.
Once erected the crane is removed. The structure takes
twelve hours to erect by six people and a total of two days

4

to set up the audio-visual equipment. The main building structure is transported in two trucks and the HVAC and interior fittings in two additional trucks. After manufacture and trial erection in Ontario, Canada, close to fabric dome manufacturers Soper's Engineered Fabric Solutions base, the building was first used in 2005 at Lincoln Plaza, New York City.

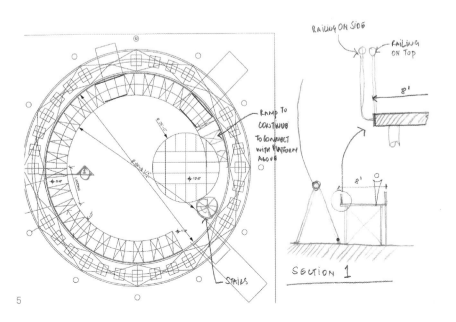

5

Toutenkamion
Screen Machine 2

2004
Designers and Constructors: Toutenkamion,
Ladon, France
Client: Highlands and Islands Arts Ltd. (Hi-Arts)

Many mobile entertainment facilities exist to provide relatively basic shelter and support facilities for large numbers of people. The driver for these structures is to provide a large venue where none exists, usually next to centres of population that will use it. However, large numbers of people live in places that are remote from the sorts of venue that city and town dwellers take for granted. It is a very different challenge to create a portable venue for small numbers that has the same quality of performance support as a permanent building built for the same purpose.

The Highlands and Islands of Scotland have a community of 360,000 people spread across a landmass larger than Belgium. First commissioned by Highlands and Islands Arts Ltd. (Hi-Arts) for use in 1999, Screen Machine is a mobile cinema that reaches out to these communities, providing them with access to full-quality 35 millimetre moving pictures. Their first mobile cinema was a specially designed, truck-based facility that was the result of a long competitive tendering process made necessary by the Scottish Arts Council funding system. The French built 'Cinemobiles' then

available did not satisfy UK legislation requirements and because of their size would not have been able to get to many of the communities they were meant to serve. The result was a compromise built on a tight budget with an uncommitted contractor who changed many of the details that were specially designed to make the facility operate efficiently. It took several hours to set up and required constant careful maintenance to keep it on the road. Nevertheless, it proved the fundamental value of the concept, giving more than 500 screenings in just four months. In 2000 and 2001, the Services Sound and Vision Corporation (SSVC) hired it for deployment to Bosnia as a service to British troops serving there. As well as film shows it provided the venue for a range of conferences and live performances, which were so successful that the Ministry of Defence funded the construction of a similar facility for its own use.

However, when it came to replacing the cinema, Hi-Arts turned to the French coach-building company, Toutenkamion (the name means 'Everything in a Truck'), to manufacture an improved version. This company has more than 20 years experience building specialist

1

2

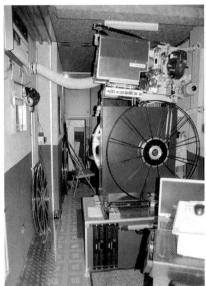

3

hybrid building/vehicles including 'Cinemobiles', mobile restaurants, recording studios, and galleries. Screen Machine 2 is based on a 17 metre long articulated trailer with its own dedicated tractor vehicle and it can travel to any location legal for a vehicle of this size. Width and height limits are normally no problem though weight sometimes can be. Once at its site, the trailer triples in size, with slide-out volumes that are supported on hydraulic legs. The interior is identical to a small screen cinema in a permanent building, with a raked auditorium, comfortable upholstered seating, and full disabled access via the external ramps and steps. Towards the cab end of the trailer is the projection room with 35 millimetre, surround sound capability. The cinema seats 102 people and is fully air-conditioned. It is important that the quality of performance is as good as a conventional cinema. The cinema takes less than 90 minutes to set up by its single driver/projectionist – ushers are hired locally. It is possible to have a matinee in one location and an evening show somewhere else, however, the screen usually stays for three to four days in each location giving up to eight screenings of three first run films.

1–3 The Screen Machine 2 deployed in Tighnabruaich, Argyle, Scotland, 2005.

AMP arquitectos/Wilk-Salinas
Bathing Ship

2005
Architect: summer version: AMP arquitectos with
Gil Wilk + Susanne Lorenz; *winter version:* Wilk-Salinas
Architekten with Thomas Freiwald
Engineer: IB Leipold, Andreas Leipold, Berlin, Germany;
Ship Engineering, HHW and partner, Wolfgang Wienecke,
Brunswick, Germany; Membrane consultants, Prof.
Dr. Wagner, Stuttgart, Germany, and Prof. Dr. Gründig
Client: Kulturarena Veranstaltungs GmbH
Location: Berlin, Germany

Berlin's River Spree has a long tradition of floating bathing facilities dating back to the nineteenth century. The *Pfuelsche Schwimmanstalt* of 1894 was a floating wooden structure built in the form of a square with the central space open to the river and the periphery arcade for changing and support spaces. The *Badeschiff* is a new bathing pool complex based on this old idea, though because of concerns about current pollution levels, the water is contained within a steel barge. The pool originally opened in 2004 as an art project created by AMP arquitectos with Gilbert Wilk and organised by the City Art Project Society of Berlin. Working with local artist Susanne Lorenz, the concept was to create a bridge to the river, reinvigorating the old idea of a mobile bath that could be placed at a different location when required. However, the new structure will be situated in the East Port area for the foreseeable future – indeed its support facilities have been built on wooden piles rather than floating structures.

The pool is contained in the hull of a 30 year old barge that is 8 metres wide by 32 metres long and 2 metres deep. It allows bathers to swim in clean water that is metaphorically, if not actually, part of the river, filtered and pumped in at a temperature of 22 degrees Celsius. A new edge was formed around the barge to contain lighting and a seat for the bathers. Though the pool is filled to the rim, the compartmented barge still contains sufficient air to float above the surface of the river. The pool was immensely popular in its first year, providing a social focus as well as a leisure activity. After its second summer a press campaign led to a €0.5 million project to make the facility both more permanent and more usable through the whole year. Wilk-Salinas were commissioned to find a charismatic yet economic solution to the problem.

The original facility consisted of three areas, two wooden parallel piers and the floating barge 'pool', all of which were open to the elements. Bathers changed and dried off in the open air, but these crude facilities were nevertheless immensely popular, with the pool staying open until midnight each evening. The decision to extend the period of use meant enclosing all three areas and this led to the opportunity to create better support facilities. The first platform now contains a reception area and a bar/café; the bridge to the next platform has toilets and showers; the second platform has a relaxation area and

1

1 The bath house fully deployed in winter mode
on the River Spree, Berlin, Germany, 2005.
2 The bath house in summer, open-air mode.

2

3/4 Interior and trial erection of the
structure in the factory.
5 Computer generated drawings
showing the form generation process
and constructional strategy.

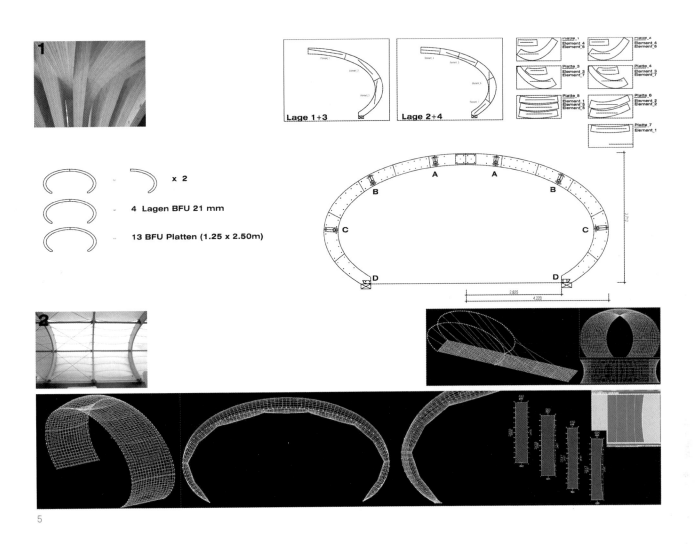

x 2

4 Lagen BFU 21 mm

13 BFU Platten (1.25 x 2.50m)

5

two saunas; a bridge leads to the barge and the pool. Waste water is taken back to the land side for disposal except for the soap-free, cold water showers' and the sauna's overflow, which is drained into the river.

The principle design feature is the twin-skin, air-filled, PVC membrane canopy roof and walls that now form a temporary skin erected in the cooler seasons. The supporting structure is a framework of prefabricated elliptical wooden trusses, made in two halves for ease of transportation and erection and bolted together at the apex on site. They are supported on a timber soleplate fixed to the edge of the platforms and the barge and are horizontally braced by five lines of steel tubes and diagonal cables in the two centre bays. Construction is simple and makes use of many standardised components and simple connections to keep costs to a minimum.

The main Ferrari membrane is translucent, however, substantial parts use a transparent Renolit material allowing views out to the river. The membranes are fixed to the end elliptical trusses by a continuous looped rope. The air-filled double-skin membrane was developed by membrane specialists schneidewind-planen and the

dry-air ventilation system engineered by Lufthig. The system took a year to develop, passing through working model and full-size mock-up stages. The cushions are fixed between the arches, twelve to each platform, 36 in total. The cushions are connected to a pressurised air tube, which in turn is connected to an air pump, which automatically maintains a constant air pressure. A demountable air-conditioning system using folding fabric ductwork keeps the air temperature at a comfortable 25 degrees Celsius even in winter. Bathers are able to swim out of the heated area of the pool below a plastic curtain and into the open air. Each summer the entire facility is returned to its basic platforms with pool – the superstructure and fittings are entirely mobile. The roof and other facilities can either be stored for the summer, or alternatively re-erected elsewhere for a shore-based pavilion. It takes three weeks to erect in October and two weeks to take apart in April/May, and is assembled and dismantled just with manual labour.

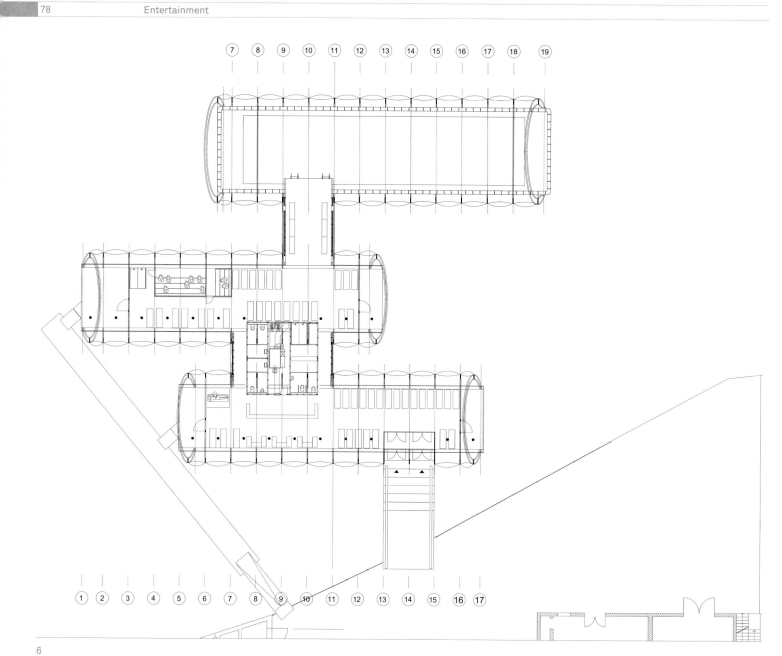

6

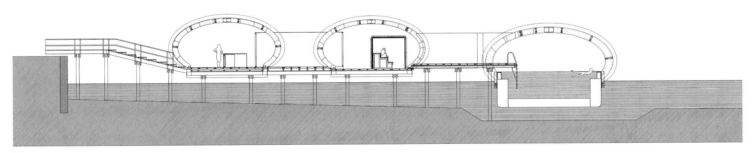

7

6 Plan.
7 Section.

Mark Fisher

U2 Vertigo Tour Stage Set
The Rolling Stones Bigger Bang Tour Stage Set
Superbowl Half-Time Shows

Mark Fisher describes himself as a technological optimist whose interest in temporary and transportable structures began during his training at the Architectural Association where he was influenced by the activities of Archigram and Cedric Price. There he created some inflatable structures that had much in common with the experimental architecture that was being produced in Europe at that time by groups such as Missing Link and Coop Himmelb(l)au. The creation of temporary stage sets for rock music events began at the beginning of the 1960s as the popularity of musicians such as Elvis Presley, the Beatles, and the Rolling Stones meant that shows began to move outside conventional concert halls into sports arenas and natural amphitheatres, sometimes in locations remote from conventional services. These early outdoor concerts used amplification and lighting designed for use in primarily static situations, however, a network of specialist companies soon emerged, developing new portable amplification, lighting, and staging techniques, and because the equipment had to be relocated for each concert, transportation, and erection services.

In 1983 architect Mark Fisher and engineer Jonathan Park formed a multi-disciplinary team to service the design aspects of stage erection. Fisher now practises independently, utilising what he describes as 'fearless' engineering from consultants such as Neil Thomas from Atelier One whom he first met when he was working for Tony Hunt (Hunt designed one of the earliest UK outdoor rock festival stages, on the Isle of Wight in 1969). His commissions for this type of work are won in much the same way as in conventional practice, in that designers are sought out because they have been involved in earlier successful projects of a similar type. Building up a good track record is important. The main clients are the musicians who are of course at the centre of the show, however, a production team with financial and operational managers is also involved from the very beginning. In this sort of project, the clients have big ambitions, which are informed by their awareness of other productions. The most important performers wish to create a bigger and better show than any done before, though in Fisher's experience they have few detailed conceptions about how this might be achieved. Usually the clients give him

1

1 U2 Vertigo Tour Stage Set
in concert mode.

a vague direction on which to develop themes and ideas
that he will then develop into a 'pitch'. Fisher designed
the seminal set for Pink Floyd's performance of 'The Wall',
given in Berlin's vast Potsdamer Platz, seen not only by
the 290,000 people present but also by a vast worldwide
television audience. Though not a mobile event it had
considerable movable elements, including a huge wall built
during the course of the show, which was then removed
at the end. He went on to design the band's Division Bell
Tour set, which established many of the strategies that
are now used for such shows.

U2 Vertigo Tour Stage Set

2005–2006
Architect: Mark Fisher, London, UK
UK engineer: MG McLaren Engineering Group,
New York, USA
Client: U2
Consultants: Art and Show Director: Willie Williams
Lighting: Patrick Woodroffe

The Vertigo Tour set for the hugely successful Irish rock
band U2 was developed out of their 2001 Elevation tour,
the band's first all-indoor tour for ten years. Fisher's
and art and show director Willie Williams' focus was to
move away from the spectacle of the previous stadium
events in order to reconnect with the band's 'raw' power.
Williams' initial idea was to bring the band into the heart
of their audience by creating a platform (literally in the
shape of a heart) that had fans gathered on all sides –
this concept was carried through intact to the final design.
There was also a concern that large-scale video projection
had taken over from the actual presence of the band as

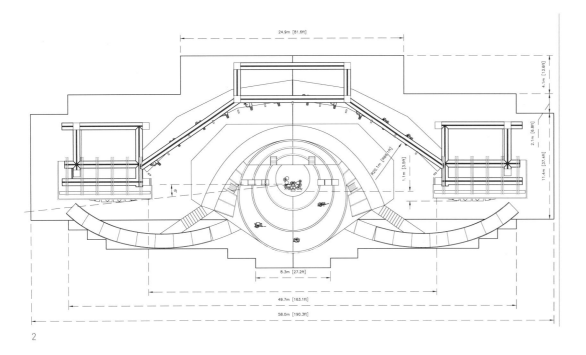

2

2 Plan.
3 U2 Vertigo Tour Stage Set.
4/5 Front elevation and section.

3

the most important feature of a U2 show, and although the idea of a no-video show was considered, the expectations of the audience and the reality of the kind of view the individual has in large venues made this impossible. Instead, a single screen was devised at a high level for each member of the band onto which were projected monochrome images throughout the show. Large-scale Pigi light show projection across the stage, the audience, and the arena walls and roof were accented on gauze screens. Paradoxically, for what was devised as a more intimate show, the tour culminated with the Superbowl 2002 half-time performance that was broad-cast live to millions around the world.

For the 2005–06 Vertigo world tour the band continued this more restrained theme, however, because the tour would also include stadium dates, things necessarily became bigger. For the earlier US dates the heart-shaped stage projecting into the audience mutated into a larger circular 'vertigo' element that also rose up around the back of the band, and for the European shows they changed again into horn-shaped catwalks that extended the same distance into the crowd with small secondary stages at

their extremity. Both projecting stages featured an LED lighting system around their edge.

A unique feature of the North American shows was the LED curtains developed by BARCO and Innovative Designs and delivered by their rental partner XL Video. The curtains are a much more sophisticated replacement for the gauze screens of the Elevation set. They consist of MiSphere LED tennis ball-sized plastic balls, which were designed specifically for the Vertigo tour. Each ball acts as a separate pixel in the string, which has 64 in each length. Their unique quality is that they are visible from every angle, giving a view from anywhere in the venue, but also having a unique view-through effect. There were a total of 189 9 metre long strings with over 12,000 individual spheres forming seven separate curtains which can be independently deployed from 5 metre long drums hoisted above the stage during the show. It takes 15 seconds to unroll the entire curtain. The entire system is comparatively quick to deploy because of the roller concept. The light and video effects were controlled by BARCO's Folsom Encore show control system, which allows a wide range of different options, separately controlling

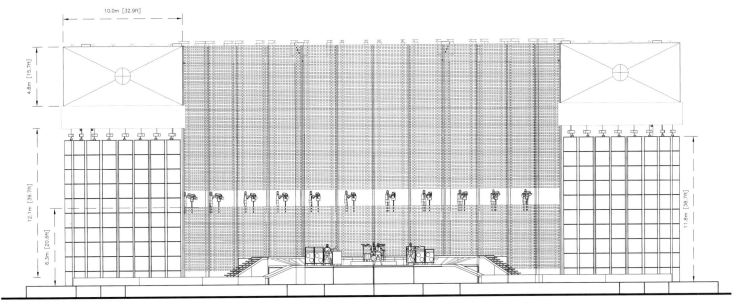

4

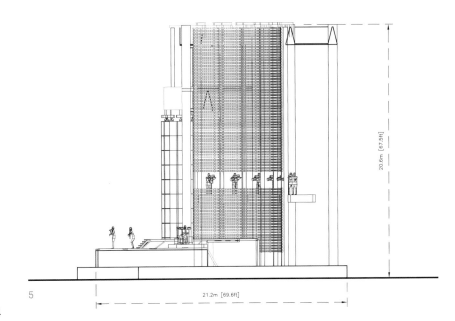

5

the screens or unifying them into a single massive entity.
Amongst the designers for the video elements was the
artist Julian Opie who created a mesmerising animated
'walking man' for the song 'Sometimes You Can't Make It
On Your Own'.

Instead of the curtains, the stadium shows used a
giant curved fixed LED screen adopted from the Popmart
tour that still, however, retained the see-through quality
of the curtain design. On either side of the LED wall a large
metal frame fronted with a bank of speakers painted in
the diagonal red and black stripe of the Vertigo album
cover was surmounted by a high-resolution video screen.
Standard structural systems provided and erected by
Tait Towers and Brilliant Stages formed the basic construction process. 80 crew members erected the set as it toured
the USA in 16 trucks and six buses. By the time the tour
was over more than four million people had seen the show
in the USA, Europe, South America, and the Far East.

1

The Rolling Stones Bigger Bang Tour Stage Set

2005–2007
Architect: Mark Fisher, London, UK
Engineer: MG McLaren Engineering Group, New York, USA
Client: The Rolling Stones; Mick Jagger and Charlie Watts
Consultants: Lighting: Patrick Woodroffe

Mark Fisher has worked on stage sets for the Rolling Stones since 1989 when he was commissioned to design the Steel Wheels tour set, which over 15 weeks attracted a total audience of three million people. The 1994 Voodoo Lounge set was erected 180 times during its twelve month long tour and it benefited from the constructional processes Fisher developed for Pink Floyd's Division Bell. In 1997, Fisher brought the final concept for the Rolling Stones' Bridges to Babylon set to fruition, interpreting ideas from a wide range of people including the band, lighting designer Patrick Woodroffe, and Jagger's friend the playwright Tom Stoppard. The end result was a visually impressive, dynamic, metamorphosing, over-the-top creation that celebrated the show's centrepiece, which

is undoubtedly the live experience of the band themselves. It was designed to follow a developing stage show with distinct phases culminating in a rousing finale. The main stage was a 'proscenium arch' structure which faced the audience, and most of the concert and the special events were based around this. The second stage was a much smaller 'club'-type structure 50 metres out in the centre of the crowd, kept a secret from the audience for the element of surprise when the band descended into their midst. The most technically demanding element in the show was the bridge that enabled the musicians to reach their island stage. This structure was not only heroic in its proportions, costing over a £1 million to manufacture, with an overall length of 52 metres and an unsupported cantilever of 43 metres, but also in its kinetic qualities – it is not a static object but extends from a secret compartment beneath the main stage. When in transit around the world, moving from aircraft hold to tour truck, and tour truck to stage, it can be driven around independently as a 15 tonne vehicle propelled by four wheel hydraulic drive and four wheel steering.

1   Rolling Stones Bigger Bang Tour Stage Set
during assembly.
2/3   Rolling Stones Bridges to Babylon Tour
Stage Set during assembly.
4   The 52 metre long deployable bridge
in use during a concert.

5

8

6

7

5–7 Rolling Stones Bigger Bang Tour
Stage Set – view before, during, and at the
culmination of the show.
8 Rolling Stones Bigger Bang Tour Stage
Set during assembly.
9 Rolling Stones Bigger Bang Tour Stage
Set plan.

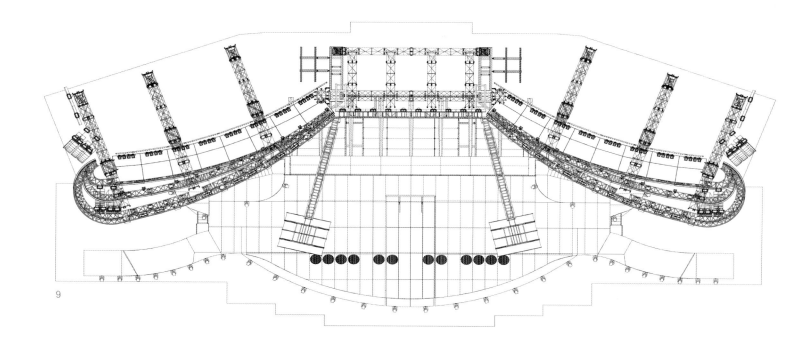

9

The Stones' A Bigger Bang show toured from August 2005 to October 2007 and included what has been suggested was the largest ever audience solely for a rock concert – two million people on Copacabana Beach, Rio de Janeiro, on February 18th 2006. 65 trucks carried two different stage set-ups that alternated between outdoor stadiums and indoor arenas. The set was the first to incorporate seats for members of the audience, based loosely on theatres like Milan's La Scala or London's Globe, with five levels of boxes with 200 seats framing each side of a giant high-resolution video screen 13 metres square (the indoor screen is a little smaller). Built using standard StageCo steel framing to support the custom aluminium support trusses, each side was 120 metres wide and 27 metres high. Two of the levels were for the lucky fans, and three for the lighting systems, though for the indoor shows the public were not admitted to the boxes, a painted backdrop giving a similar effect to the main audience. The balconies were faced with 90 composite fibreglass panels containing an LED lighting system and behind these were two 21 by 15 metre low-resolution video screens. In what has now become a regular requirement, the band

wished to have a closer relationship with the main audience for part of the show. A pier-like structure enabled Jagger to strut out above the crowd; however, this ramp was also used for one of the show's key elements. Fisher created a dramatic transformation in which the centre part of the stage detached from the main area and moved along the pier under its own power 120 metres out into the arena.

The usual pyrotechnics were supplemented by a giant 'Lips' inflatable and a flame machine that operated during the Stones' song 'Sympathy for the Devil'. The sophistication of the lighting systems devised by Patrick Woodroffe was key to creating the look of the show. A wide range of different types, colours, and power levels were incorporated into an extremely complex computer-controlled system, effectively giving each song its own unique lighting performance. The fittings were colour coded to ensure they were always deployed in the correct location.

Superbowl Half-Time Shows

2001, 2002, 2004, 2006
Architect: Mark Fisher, London, UK
Set Engineer: MG McLaren Engineering Group,
New York, USA
Client: MTV

Construction and operation strategies often have to be very different for portable building construction. A particularly difficult logistical problem solved by Mark Fisher has been how to create a complete stage with amplification and lighting rigs that spans the 45 metre width of a football field in four and a half minutes. For client MTV, Fisher has created completely demountable systems that can be erected solely with human power during the Superbowl half-time intervals. As the players leave the field the vast team (usually more than 400 volunteers) runs on carrying the structure's components. In 2001 they erected an 18 metre high structure in front of the 78,000 audience during the four and a half minute television commercial break. The ensuing show by NSYNC

and Aerosmith was seen on live television by an estimated 115 million people.

In 2002 the U2 show reproduced the heart-shaped stage used for the band's current Elevation tour. The 24 metre by 30 metre stage was surmounted by a 60 metre long diamond-shaped lighting grid. Towards the end of the show an 18 metre by 46 metre kabuki curtain descended as a screen onto which the names of the victims of the terrorist attack of 11th September 2001 were projected. Dramatically, it fell to the ground at the end of the performance, apparently dematerialising the names into the air. The 2004 show featured Justin Timberlake and Janet Jackson (whose wardrobe famously 'malfunctioned') performing on Fisher's most complex stage to date. 26 carts were manoeuvered to the centre of the football field containing lifts, balloon screens, telescoping towers, and the six 9 metre hinging 'tusks' on which dancers performed. The show lasted just twelve minutes but included five act changeovers and five technical set-changes seamlessly accomplished in front of a live crowd of 70,000 people. The Rolling Stones featured in the 2006 show performing on a stage in the shape of the band's 'Lips' logo

7

made from mobile carts. Movable lighting rigs, pyrotechnics, drop-down fabric panels, and an 'instant' floor-level
crowd of 3,000 in addition to the stadium audience created
an effective event with relatively simple constructional
elements. Though not mobile in the sense of being relocated from place to place, the components of these shows
are portable in that they must be moved into position
very quickly from outside the stadium to centre stage in
just a few minutes.

Vastly different memorable events and effects can
be created relatively quickly and economically by utilising
standard systems and experienced contractors such as
Tait Towers who are also involved in the touring stage
shows. The proof of the success of Fisher's work is that his
clients return to him for his conceptual and detailed design
skills. As well as the Rolling Stones, Pink Floyd, and U2 he
has worked for Simply Red, Bryan Adams, Whitney Houston,
Tina Turner, Janet Jackson, Jean-Michel Jarre, George
Michael, Robbie Williams, and Stevie Wonder. Fisher has
also worked on other projects in related fields such as the
'Wizard of Oz' ice show devised by Barnum and Bailey and
the Ringling Brothers which toured for five years giving

more than 3,000 performances throughout North and
South America, the Pacific, and Europe.

The relationship between the creation of spectacular
transportable stage sets and conventional architecture
is complex. It is obvious that the sets have substantial
architectural presence, use many of the same inspirations
in their formal design, and are seen by many thousands
of people, however, it could be argued (and Fisher makes
this point himself) that these designs are essentially
two-dimensional, they are meant to be viewed by the
audience, not used by them. The people who use the sets
are the musicians and those who prepare the show.
Ancillary accommodation such as toilets, showers, cater-
ing, wardrobe, make-up, and video production suites
are provided by portable trailers or specially designed
vehicles. The actual sets modify their environments in a
primarily visual and aural manner but other environmental
interventions are minimal, such as basic shelter from the
rain for delicate equipment. These great touring shows are
generally a summer event, when better weather can be
relied on during the concert and erection and dismantling
procedures. Though they are technically complex and

8

8 NFL Superbowl 2004 half-time show featuring Janet Jackson and Justin Timberlake.
9/10 NFL Superbowl 2004 half-time show
during assembly and performance.
11/12 NFL Superbowl 2006 half-time
show featuring the Rolling Stones during
practice assembly.

often innovative in the use of lighting, video projection techniques, and computer-controlled effects, they are loosely fitted into the set in order to allow quick assembly and dismantling and are therefore not fine-tuned in the sense that the services of a building are. These stage sets are not critically inspected at close quarters but seen, often from a single viewpoint, from comparatively long distances. Fisher makes the point that in an age of such sophisticated technology the link between form and function has become obscured and in fact unnecessary – set structures can take any form, the more unusual the better, in order to achieve their main function of communication of a dramatic image related to the performers' musical and artistic ideas. In essence, all rock sets have the same programme though their appearance may be radically different. In an industry where everything should at least appear fresh each time, it is often the rearrangement of standard components rather than the introduction of new ones that gives that impression. However, Fisher still believes that as in architecture, the quality of structure and form is reinforced if they are consistent and synonymous.

The budget for the projects is usually firmly established before design begins and the manufacture of the set, which may cost as much as $4 million (though the Potsdamer Platz show cost $10 million) with up to half of that spent on special customised scenery, may only be a relatively small part of the total budget. Approximately $0.5 million is spent on the presentation of each show with a complete tour costing $25 million or more. Cost control experts are appointed on a project basis in much the same way as the designer, and they also move from tour to tour in the same way. Contracts are not as complex as in conventional construction, often by letters of agreement based on a set of drawings, which are less detailed than in the building industry. Because there is a great deal of repetitive work, contractors are familiar with the working methods and operation pattern of companies they have collaborated with before and this leads to mutual trust.

There are significant differences between the design of these large transportable stage sets and conventional construction. Many of the systems which are used have arisen specifically from the nature of the task and been

9

10

11

12

developed within the industry, though it is clearly possible that they might also be of use in the erection of conventional building projects. The time scale for creating these sets is often telescoped, four months from design concept to completion is common. For this reason many of the usual attributes of conventional building are inappropriate. The production manager, lighting and effects designers, even the master rigger who will govern the erection team, take part in the design process from the very beginning. The use of specialist experience is crucial, not just that of engineers like Neil Thomas who have a knowledge of new materials and techniques, but also that of specialist manufacturers and erection companies like the Belgian organisation StageCo who provided standard components and erection services for the Bigger Bang set and many others. A process concerned with the concept of what Americans call 'value engineering' is used, in which all those involved in the different areas that make up the show are involved in its overall design. The objective is to ensure that the constructional and logistical strategies that are most effective are coordinated for ultimate efficiency. Though each show must be unique, many standard components are used, though these may have been specially developed for the industry, often by the people who supply and erect them. A series of very experienced companies who are used to working with each other often bid for the same jobs and are familiar with the logistics of their task. Despite the short lead-in time, by the end of each job Fisher will often know by name each of the crew working on a particular project. This is a common feature of the relationships created during this sort of project and mutual trust and an understanding of the capabilities and the requirements of each team member's role are an essential feature in the tour's efficient operation. Even though many pre-manufactured standard components are used, handicraft is still important, both in the preparation period when special scene assembly, inflatable manufacture, and lighting effects are made, but also as the show travels on the road, when solutions to the inevitable running problems must be found on site, at short notice. In essence, the philosophy that the show must go on is as important for one as technologically complex as this as it has been in the past.

FTL Design Engineering Studio

Harley-Davidson Machine Tent

2002
Architect/Engineer: FTL Design Engineering Studio,
New York, USA
Client: Harley-Davidson Motorcycles

The 'Machine Tent' for the Harley-Davidson Travelling Tour (celebrating the motorcycle manufacturer's 100th anniversary in 2002) was the only custom-designed component in a large travelling show that travelled throughout the USA and to Tokyo, Sydney, Cologne, Mexico City, Vancouver, and Barcelona. The challenge was to make a structure that could accommodate the varying building codes and erection conditions in these different parts of the world but also meet a deadline requiring all design, engineering, and construction to be completed in under 20 weeks.

The solution was a 50 metre diameter building that could be erected in just three days without the use of heavy cranes or other equipment. The building consists of a central mast and six secondary masts that all have internally mounted winches, which haul up all the required elevated components. The curving segment that caps the secondary masts creates an internal element reminiscent of the motorcycle structures exhibited below, but also provides the building's unique external form. The elements that compose the six fields of the circular design are all identical to allow for quick and easy assembly. Although

it uses the latest technology the building sits firmly within the tradition of the circus tent, reinvigorating it with contemporary meaning. After the tour was completed in 2003 a rental company purchased the tent from Harley-Davidson to use for other events.

Though tents are an archetypal mobile architectural form, developments in materials technology, coupled with the raised ambitions of clients, have led to much more sophisticated solutions. Advanced computer-aided design methods coupled with increased performance fabrics that are stronger, more flexible, and more stable can result in larger buildings that require less structure. The character of the exterior form and interior lighting conditions can now be manipulated in complex ways resulting in more satisfactory building solutions. Over three decades of design practice FTL Design Engineering Studio have produced some of the most innovative buildings of this type – transferring innovations between permanent and mobile projects, dedicated and commercial solutions. Their aim is not to create buildings that look specifically portable, but rather to convey in their imagery the nature of the structural system and

1

1/2 FTL Design Engineering Studio's
Machine Tent for Harley-Davidson's
Travelling Tour, 2002.

the dynamic qualities of the materials utilised to
achieve their purpose. Mobility is not something that
has dictated the entire concept but simply a part of
the response to a complex architectural brief that has
led to the ultimate solution.

2

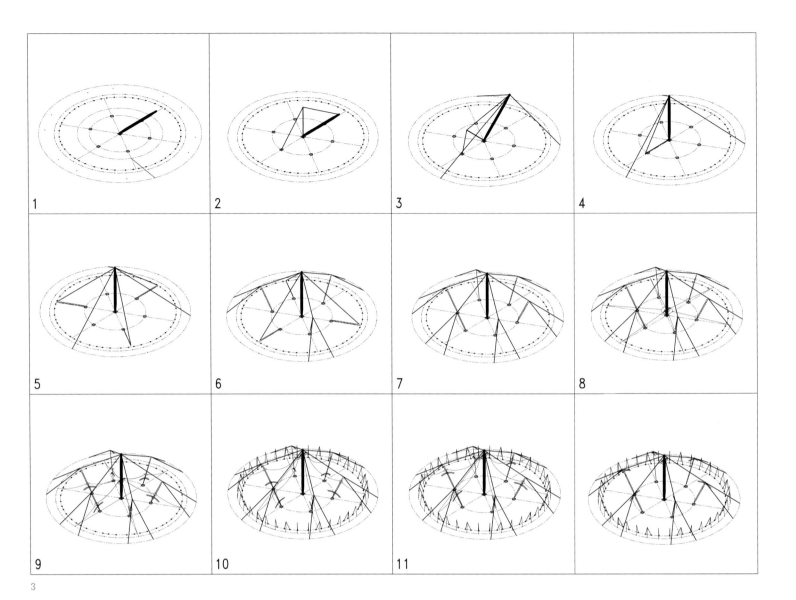

3

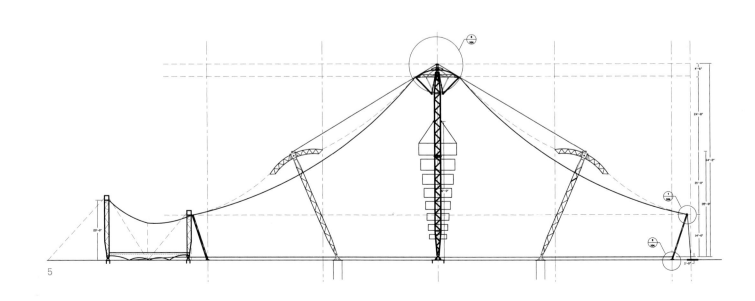

5

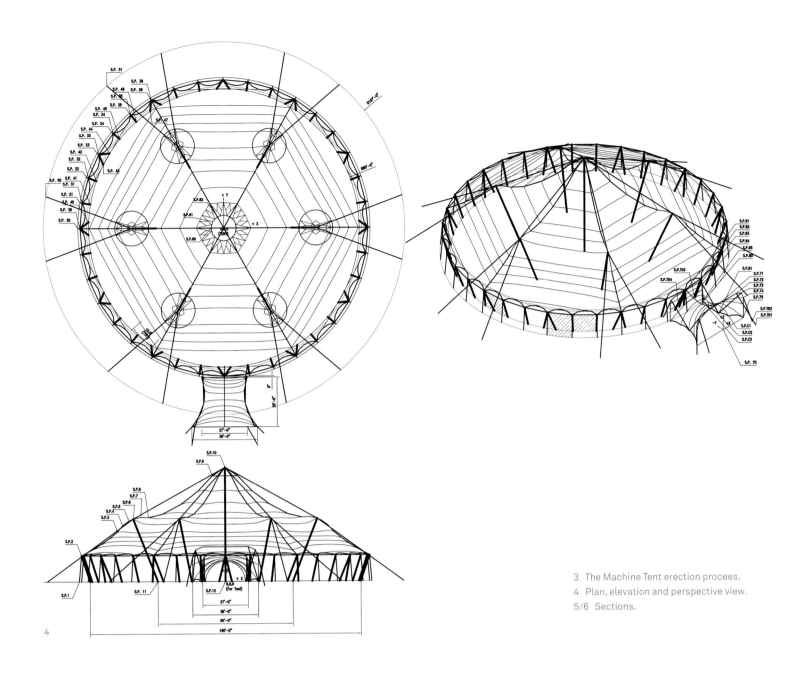

3   The Machine Tent erection process.
4   Plan, elevation and perspective view.
5/6   Sections.

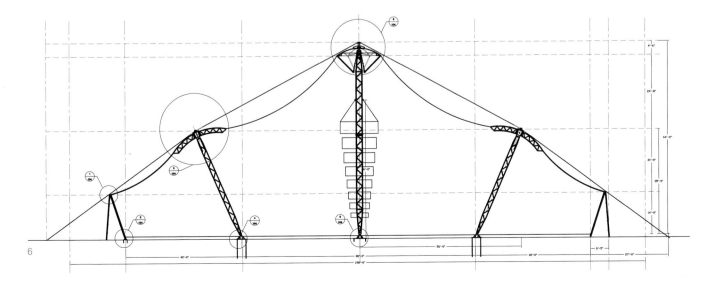

Rudi Enos
Valhalla

2000
Client and Designer: Gearhouse Structures, Rudi Enos, Bruno Postle, Stuart Holdsworth, Jade Dearling, Sheffield, UK
Consultants: Special Structures Lab Ltd., Sheffield, UK

The circus tent is the definitive mobile entertainment building. The form and material of this structure is synonymous with large-scale temporary venues – it is a very efficient method of covering large areas because it is lightweight and relatively quick and easy to erect. These factors are equally true for non-portable structures and it is therefore not surprising that membrane structures are increasingly used for permanent large-scale entertainment projects. The most high-profile building of this type in the UK is the Millennium Experience Dome, which owes its form, its construction, its use of materials, and its structural systems to portable building precedents. It was designed by architects Richard Rogers Partnership, and consulting engineers Buro Happold. The building consists of a Sheerfill PTFE-coated, fabric-clad, stressed cable dome supported by twelve main columns. It is big – 320 metres in diameter, over 100 metres to the top of the masts and more than 1,000 metres around its circumference. An internal Fabrasorb lining is used as insulation to mitigate condensation problems. The dome possesses the archetypal image of that quintessential movable pleasure dome: the circus – its form, its construction, its

structure, perhaps its very existence would not have happened without such historical and contemporary portable architecture precedents. In 2007, the dome reopened, rebranded as the O_2 Arena, containing a 20,000 seat venue for sport, concerts and events, a 2,500 seat music and theatre amphitheatre, an exhibition space, an eleven screen cinema, restaurants, and bars, with planned future development including a hotel and conference base.

The Millennium celebrations also provided the impetus to create the Valhalla tent, which is the largest mobile membrane structure in the world. Concept designer Rudi Enos had previous experience creating mobile tents for the 'Walt Disney on Ice' show and the rental Kayam Theatre, which was later used by the band Radiohead for the first UK rock tour to take place in a portable venue. Though not as large as the Millennium Dome, Valhalla is still construction on an enormous scale with a total area of 23,456 square metres and an internal span of 75 metres. On the first night the £1.26 million building was used (millennium eve), it hosted a party for 28,000 people generating a revenue of £4 million. Enos' intention was to create a sense of wonder for those who enter the building and so he

1

1   Valhalla tent aerial view.

named Valhalla after the mythical hall in Asgard belonging to the Norse god Odin, which in legend had 540 doors, each large enough to allow 800 warriors to enter abreast.

During 1997 and 1998 Enos carried out extensive engineering analysis to create the main design and check its operational safety, developing 90 % of the design's key parameters. Bruno Postle then ensured that it worked in terms of geometry and possessed sufficient tolerances to operate in the desired manner, and developed the form-finding and connection details. Stuart Holdsworth focused on portability factors whilst also making sure that engineering and safety standards were met. Jade Dearling was influential on the design of the erection process and rigging design.

The design of Valhalla began by establishing stringent constructional and operational criteria to make sure that the building could fulfil its purpose whilst still being economically viable to construct and use. Flexibility was a key factor: the building being designed to be used in different configurations dependant on demand, but also having a form and layout that did not compromise its operation. There is a 30 metre span between the kingpost mast supports, and the perimeter has 6 metre high side-walls. Valhalla's smallest operating size uses a single mast and is 45 metres on each side (2,025 square metres), but by adding 25 metre wide sections the size can be expanded to the maximum, which has 20 masts. This flexibility not only allows clients to rent the size of venue that they require but also means that the components are in use and therefore generating revenue more continuously. It was also decided that each pair of masts could support an additional load of 200 kilonewtons for event equipment such as lighting, effects, and amplification. 30 by 2.2 by 1.5 metre trusses span between the masts to support this equipment. These fold down flat and are split into sections 10 metres long and 30 centimetres wide for transportation. Three 4.5 kilowatt motors are located in each pair of masts to lift the trusses and the membranes via a system of wire ropes and pulleys. Hand-held, low-voltage remote controls operate the system, which includes over 2,000 metres of galvanised and pre-stretched cable used to stabilise the structure during and after erection.

The Valhalla membrane was designed using in-house visualisation and patterning software 'Patterner', developed

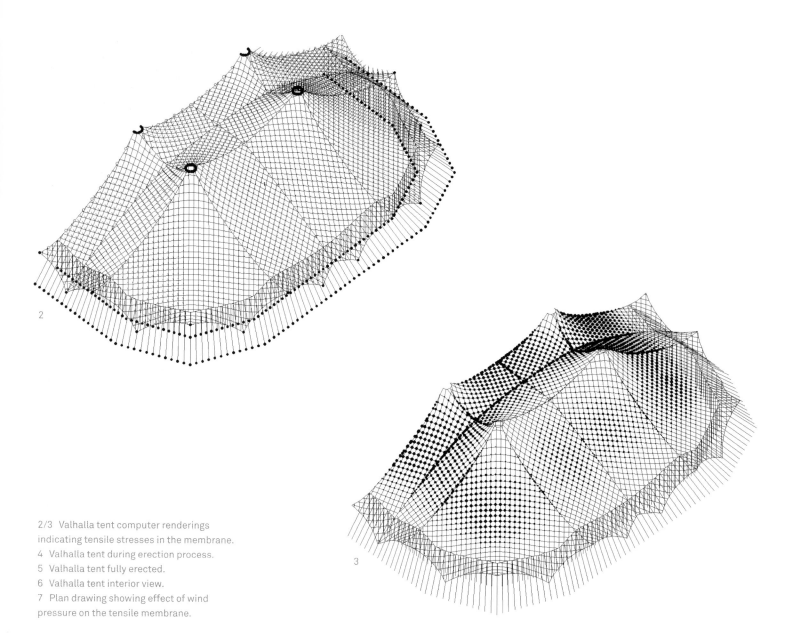

2/3 Valhalla tent computer renderings
indicating tensile stresses in the membrane.
4 Valhalla tent during erection process.
5 Valhalla tent fully erected.
6 Valhalla tent interior view.
7 Plan drawing showing effect of wind
pressure on the tensile membrane.

by Bruno Postle. Tech-net 'EASY' software was used to establish membrane forces and cable analysis and to determine maximum loads, deflections, and reaction loads. Every possible situation was modelled to make sure the structure was both efficient and safe and was able to meet appropriate regulation standards and codes of practice. The membrane has 4,500 kilogramme PVC-coated webbing radio frequency welded onto each panel, creating a radial net of reinforcement around the entire structure. No wire cables are used in the membrane because of their weight, their lack of flexibility, and the danger of chafing. Instead, a system of 10 centimetre wide webbings connect the membranes together. These are sealed by a rain cover, which can be either opaque or translucent giving the flexibility of a well lit or fully controllable blackout interior. Valhalla has experienced every sort of weather during its deployment history, high winds, heavy rain, and snow, but as the structure is engineered to cope with the most extreme conditions plus a large factor of safety, no problems have been encountered.

The entire structure is transported in ten standard ISO containers, which include all components including the masts – smaller versions use fewer containers. The form of the building, with its steep curved rising roof is not only dramatic but also structurally efficient, utilising optimum membrane forms (except at the ends where the short span made a flatter shape more practical). The structure is assembled entirely without cranes and does not use extensive groundworks in order to maintain optimum mobility. Valhalla can be erected with just twelve operatives in three days using telescopic forklift trucks. The first task is to lay out the king pole masts which have the motors and rigging connected and in place. The poles are brought to the vertical and the lifting rings brought to a position half way up. The outer 'A' frame masts are connected to the membrane and partly raised – the membrane is then checked to make sure all its connections are correct before theses masts are raised to their final position. The membrane is then hoisted to its final height and all the tiebacks are checked for the correct tension. Valhalla uses 2 metre long screw ground anchors, which are tested with a torque meter to ensure they will meet the required load of up to 280 kilonewtons. The lifting gear is then secured and electrical connections

4

5

6

to the winches removed before interior fit-out and perimeter walls are installed.

Valhalla is of course remarkable for its scale, but also because of the logistical systems employed in its operation, which makes it efficient to use for a great variety of events and clients, including the main exhibition hall for the Earth Summit in Johannesburg, South Africa, in 2002. Ten years after its design it is still the largest portable structure to be in operation and this is due to its speed of erection, its economy in operation, and its capacity to operate in a wide range of environmental conditions. Buildings that are required to be relocated from place to place need to be relocated easily and economically even at this size, however, the value of having such a massive structure available for temporary events in almost any location is clear.

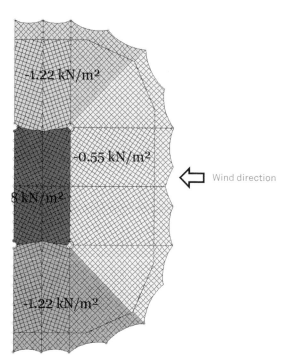

-1.22 kN/m²

-0.55 kN/m²   ⇐ Wind direction

8 kN/m²

-1.22 kN/m²

7

Office of Mobile Design
Portable House

2007
Architect: Office of Mobile Design, Venice, USA;
Jennifer Siegal; Mark Stankard

The possibilities of adapting materials and construction techniques from other industries such as aerospace and car manufacture have been advocated by many commentators since the beginning of the twentieth century and though many exciting prototypes exist, the full impact of widespread technology transfer has yet to be exploited. Portable architecture uses some of the most innovative forms of building yet devised, which makes it a valuable testing ground for the rest of the industry. One example is manufactured building, which utilises factory production techniques to provide high-quality buildings at low cost. The mobile home industry provides a quarter of all new houses in North America, with factory-made buildings that are transported either as completed dwellings or as double-wides, which are joined together on site. Architects in the USA and Europe are now engaged in utilising the methods of this industry to create alternative housing designs. The 1994 competition-winning house designed by Abacus architects utilised existing mobile home construction techniques to develop a high-quality, low-cost prototype home that was built on a production line in three weeks, delivered to site for assembly, and ready for occupation two and a half weeks later. There has also been considerable recent interest in the UK regarding the potential of prefabricated techniques to solve the parallel problems of too few homes being available at too high a cost. For example, architects Cartwright Pickard, in collaboration with clients The Peabody Trust and manufacturers Yorkon (a part of the Portakabin group), are one of several groups involved in designing high-quality housing based on the strategy of factory-built modules that are then transported to site in order to reduce construction time significantly.

Jennifer Siegal's Office of Mobile Design (OMD) is based in Los Angeles, California. The majority of OMD'S built work has involved community and education agencies and Siegal is an advocate of the do-it-yourself, self-help approach to creating buildings. OMD's range of speculative work is wide, from mobile shops and information technology centres to community-based mobile educational facilities.

OMD's Portable House is a redesign of the typical North American mobile home that incorporates conventional manufactured housing construction techniques

1/2 Office of Mobile Design Portable House,
computer generated images.

3

4

3 Single module unit exterior.
4 Single module unit en-route to site in
Los Angeles, USA.
5/6 Plan and elevations of the standard
single module unit.

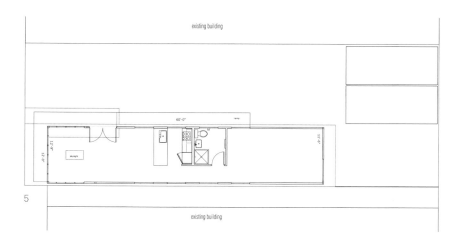

5

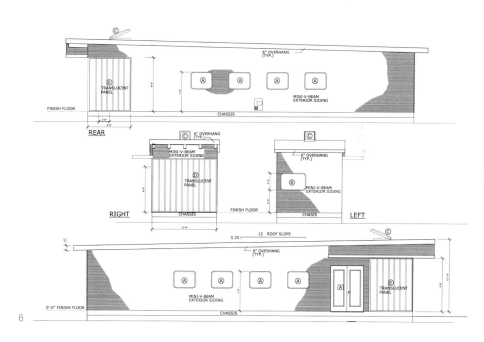

6

with a contemporary design aesthetic and an ecological emphasis. Because they are factory-made they are economic to produce and consequently relatively cheap to buy, however, for the same reason they are also constructed to a higher standard utilising repetitive, standardised methods and materials. The basic module's steel frame structure is 3.6 metres by 18 metres, though much of the secondary framing is timber from renewable resources. It is clad externally with metal siding and translucent polycarbonate panels and internally with sustainable floor and wall materials. These include: Durapalm, a non-wood flooring material made from Asian coconut palms; Plyboo®, a bamboo flooring system; Wheatsheet, made of recycled wheat fibres and used in walls as an alternative to particleboard and medium density fibreboard (MDF). Kirei Board, made from the discarded stalks of the sorghum plant and non-toxic KR Bond glue is used in the manufacture of a composite panel board. Although the showhouse is in the form of a single-wide unit with a 70 square metre area, it has been designed as part of a modular system that can accommodate many variations. For example, an eight-module version proposed for a site in Encinitas, California, is more than 400 metres square on two storeys and has four bedrooms and a double garage.

The Portable House modules are made by the mobile home manufacturer Brandall Manufacturing, one hour from Los Angeles. Siegal has been working with the company for five years developing the possibilities for using new materials and design concepts into their manufacturing process. The home takes four to eight weeks to construct depending on specification and is trucked to site fully-assembled, including a fitted kitchen and bathroom, and heating and ventilating systems. It is much quicker to build, is capable of relocation, and costs about 15% less than a comparable conventionally built house. On-site installation for the single module ShowHouse Portable Home took only two hours, although installation of the two-storey variants is far more complex with multiple service connections and joints between rooms and floors. In the Pacific Palisades area of Los Angeles OMD have built a large 300 metre square house with six modules that is fitted into a tight urban site. The six modules were built independently in the factory

7

8

and, after the laying of concrete foundations and building in service connections, they were assembled on site with the use of a crane. Cladding was installed after installation of the modules though much of the interior was completed in the factory. Though it is relatively easy to resite the single module buildings, these more complex projects are unlikely to be moved once installed, although the potential does exist.

9

10

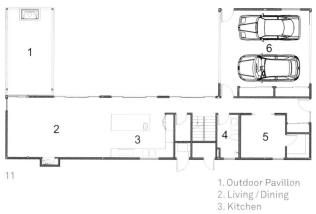

11

1. Outdoor Pavillon
2. Living / Dining
3. Kitchen
4. Bathroom
5. Study
6. Garage

13

12

1. Terrace
2. Master Bedroom
3. Master Bedroom
4. Laundry
5. Playroom
6. Bathroom
7. Bedroom

7/8 Single module unit interior.
9 Multi-module unit under construction.
10 CAD image of the design for the
completed multi-module unit.
11/12 First floor plan, and second floor plan.
13 Section.

Richard Horden

micro-compact home

2005
Architects: Horden Cherry Lee Architects, London, UK;
Richard Horden; Haack + Höpfner, Munich; Lydia Haack
Consultants: Concept and Development: TU Munich,
Richard Horden
Production: m-ch, micro-compact home
Production GmbH

The architect's house is understandably recognised as a vehicle for expression and experimentation both by its designer and by those interested in the implementation of innovation in building design. The house is a universally understood (and often underestimated) design problem and this means that innovative solutions are more clearly understood by observers. The problem of the dwelling is of course influenced dramatically by its relationship to culture and society, however, it is also perceived by designers as an unending and intriguing problem. Buckminster Fuller's Dymaxion dwelling project for an economical demountable housing solution achieved through mass-production and industrialisation, though not realised, is just one example of the many precedents in this area. Some designers have spread their search for applied, transferable, technological systems into other industries, with the direct purpose of finding new ways of building truly contemporary houses. This has become more than just a search for appropriate alternative production techniques, and also involves exploiting their inherent value in technical and aesthetic terms. Although the intention for these projects has usually been to develop new ideas

for permanent building, it has also in some cases led the designers to question the necessity of a permanent location for the contemporary dwelling.

Richard Horden's innovative yacht house projects incorporate the products and assembly techniques of the lightweight technology developed for the manufacture of yachts. Horden's influences have been described as hang gliders, Tensegrity sculptures, and especially his own Tornado catamaran sailing yacht, which can be assembled and dismantled in an hour. He makes the point that modern boats are lightweight, strong, corrosion-free vessels that compare favourably to wet construction with steel and bricks. Horden has used yacht components made by Proctor Masts to make buildings as these components have been designed to accommodate the requirements of a kinetic object powered by dynamic forces. His first house of this type was built in Woodgreen, New Forest, UK, in 1984. Made from an assemblage of recognisable yacht components, it resulted in a transferred yet fresh image. In their normal situation such components are required to be regularly assembled, disassembled, and reassembled depending on the direction and state of the wind and the

1   Seven unit micro-compact home
complex in the *Englischer Garten*, Munich,
Germany, 2005.

yacht. Used for a new purpose, they lend buildings a sense of lightness and dynamism that retains the richness that domestic design requires.

Buildings made primarily from components such as this are assembled as a series of simple and separate sequences. After the foundations are made the masts and spars are erected into an independent framework into which prefabricated roof and wall panels are fixed. Horden has used the technology of yacht manufacture to produce a kit of parts that can be easily assembled with unskilled labour. Horden's ultimate portable building designed using this system is the air-lifted alpine shelter, the SkiHaus, which utilises similar components to the yacht houses.

micro-compact home

Richard Horden's role as a professor in the Institute of Architecture and Product Design at the Technical University (TU) Munich has resulted in a series of experimental projects under the banner 'micro-architecture', buildings and objects designed to be beautifully crafted, economic in materials, lightweight, and flexible. Collaborating with students and staff at the university, Horden has created

a number of viable projects – quite often tested full size, with a few coming to production. The most ambitious of these is the micro-compact home (m-ch), designed as an affordable, mobile, temporary house that is completely uncompromising in terms of the quality of design, construction, and fittings. Inspired by the scale and order of the classical Japanese teahouse, though utilising the latest contemporary technology, the initial design stages were informed by collaboration between TU Munich and the Tokyo Institute of Technology. Initially called the i-home, the first design mock-up used for testing the concept was completed by staff and students at TU Munich. The development and realisation of a first prototype was undertaken by Horden Cherry Lee together with Lydia Haack + John Höpfner Architekten as part of a commission from the Verein Studentenstadt München e.V. (Mr Dieter Maßberg) and was sponsored by O_2 Germany. In a second stage, the first 'serialisation' was undertaken, the O_2 Village in Munich-Freimann, near to the Englische Garten. Since November 2005, the 'mini-homes' are now occupied by students studying a variety of different subjects.

2

3

The technological objective of the m-ch is to bring advanced construction systems together with a harmonious sophisticated contemporary environment. Everything required in a conventional home is provided within a cube 2.66 metre square, which makes up for lack of floor area with ingenious multi-use spaces. Internal ceiling height is 1.89 metres and the volume is 18.6 cubic metres. Surprisingly, the unit contains two beds (1.98 by 1.05 metres), a sitting area, a 1.05 by 0.65 metre table for work and dining, a shower and toilet cubicle, a kitchen plus multiple storage compartments for clothes, possessions, and food. Not surprisingly, the design emphasis with such a small, multi-functional environment is on efficiency and simplicity. One bed folds up into the wall whilst a second can be made in the seating area after folding the table. The m-ch uses high-quality fixtures and fittings that are adapted from automotive, marine, and aviation technologies such as LED light fittings, ducted warm-air heating and air-conditioning. Also included in the price are a double induction hob, oven, microwave, fridge and freezer, three-bin recycling waste system, and two flat-screen televisions. The m-ch should use only 350 kilowatt

hours per month in a cold winter and 120 kilowatt hours in the summer, including air-conditioning.

The m-ch is constructed by Gatterbauer in their Austrian factory. The company's previous experience was in manufacturing glass, aluminium, and timber conservatories. Complete factory construction enables strict control to be maintained during assembly to provide the highest quality finish. The m-ch is made with a recyclable timber-frame panel construction clad in flat anodised aluminium cladding and a PVC inner lining. The floor finish is epoxy and the opening surfaces are aluminium. Window frames are double glazed aluminium frame units. Roof insulation is a vacuum system chosen for its high efficiency and light weight. The site needs to be prepared for service connections although foundations are minimal due to the comparative light weight of the building (2.2 tonnes). Installation is incredibly simple, the unit being crane lifted from the back of a truck and dropped into place – connection to services takes literally five minutes. A range of further optional accessories is available including an external deck and a ski store. A low-energy version is also available which is powered by an 8 square

4

2/3 Deployment by crane in
a confined space.
4 Interior – kitchen to left, living/
sleeping area to right.

metre photovoltaic solar panel and a small diameter vertical axis wind generator. Calculations suggest that located
in the UK the home would be energy neutral in winter and
would generate more than 1,000 kilowatt hours per month
in summer.

Because the cost of the m-ch is far less than a conventional house it is proposed that an individual might
exchange ownership of one large house for several that are
much smaller. These could be located close to work or
leisure interests – in the city for business, in the country
for rest, in a manufacturing area for work, in the mountains
for sport. The mode of delivery and the minimal site intervention means that the building can fit into remote and
sensitive sites, and trial deployments have already been
made. Up to five units can be delivered on a single truck,
which can crane it in up to 40 metres away from a road.
In extreme situations the m-ch can also be delivered
by helicopter. To buy a m-ch costs about the same as a
medium-sized caravan (though purchase of land, site
preparation, and connection are extra), however, its inten-
tions are quite different. Its small size is used to great
advantage in many ways – efficiency in use of materials,

in heating and cooling, in transportation and deployment
costs, but most of all in its ability to be located in a vast
range of locations. Its design objectives are also quite
different and uncompromised by the small size. The m-ch
is intended to be a real house, built to the highest standards, including the latest technology – the quality of
thought that has gone into detailed design is essential
because providing such a sophisticated level of operation
in such a compact space is difficult to do, but also so
that its quality is sufficient to meet the aspirations of its
target audience.

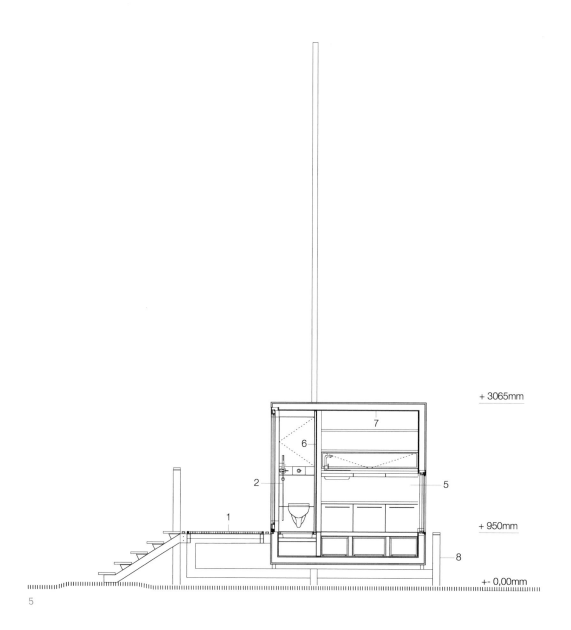

+ 3065mm

+ 950mm

+- 0,00mm

5

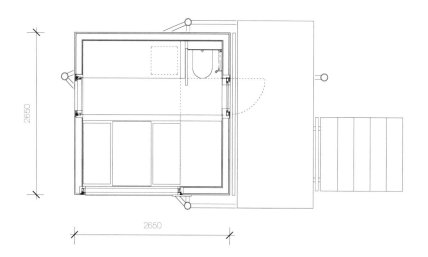

5 Plan and section.
6 Plan of multi-unit complex.

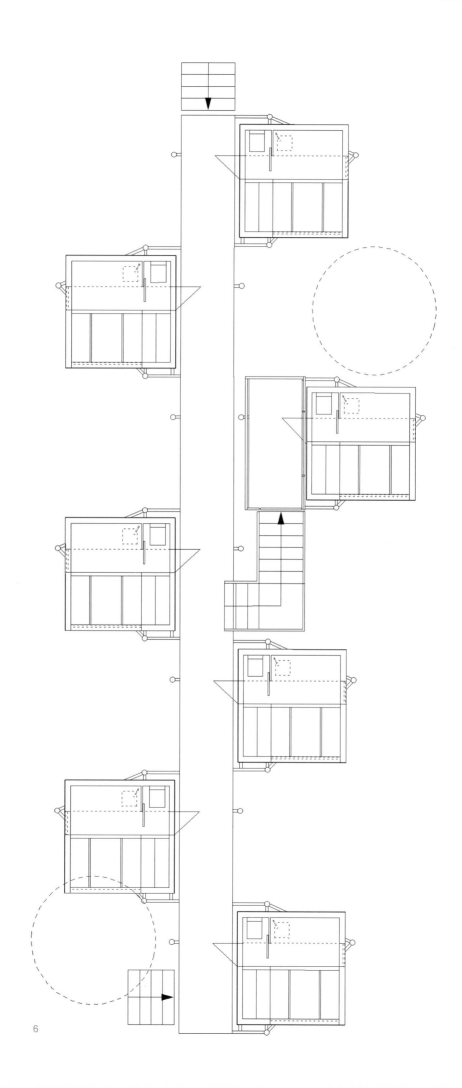

6

Paul Burchill and Hervé Delaby
Caravan of the Future

2007
Designers: Paul Burchill and Hervé Delaby
Constructors: Bailey Caravans, Bristol, UK
Client: The Caravan Club

The Caravan Club is Europe's largest caravanning association representing one million enthusiasts. For its centenary celebrations the Club commissioned a competition to find a new approach to caravan design. The brief was to design the caravan of the future with the ambition that the chosen design would be built. Inspiration for the winner came from classic aircraft shapes such as the Douglas DC3 and contemporary curving car design like the recent Volkswagen Beetle. Its name, Cargo S, acknowledges the French word for a snail, 'escargot'. At 5 metres long by 2.5 metres wide this caravan is broadly similar in plan dimensions to a typical European towing caravan, however, at 3 metres high it is taller, providing a less enclosed feeling. Suitability for towing is a big factor in caravan design. By minimising towing size, prioritising an aerodynamic shape, and providing expanding units to extend the space once in situ, an easily towable trailer can be converted into a larger living space.

Because of restrictions on the amount of time available to build it, the prototype was constructed as a test-bed for ideas about form and usability rather than use on the open road. Though innovative in layout and, to a certain extent, form, the prototype was built using conventional caravan construction. A standard Al-Ko caravan chassis formed the base onto which a two-tier laminated sandwich panel was attached – this had to be strong enough to take the sliding/folding extension pieces as well as the normal floor and fittings load. The side panels were formed from flat aluminium bonded panels fixed to specially shaped, curved GRP sections at the edges. A strong lattice timber frame was erected to support the hemispherical roof and provide rigidity. The shell was completed with specially made acrylic windows before being spray-painted. The extending sections, which house bunks and a seating area, were fitted next. The interior fittings were all based on existing caravan components although they were specially constructed to closely match the design proposals. Caravans, although built on a production line, are still largely hand-built and this was the case with the Cargo S, taking 1,000 man-hours to complete.

1

2

1/2 Exterior and interior in deployed form.

LOT-EK
Mobile Dwelling Unit

2003
Architect: LOT-EK, Giuseppe Lignano and Ada Tolla,
New York, USA
Client: Walker Art Center and Art Museum of the
University of Santa Barbara

Like many of LOT-EK's commercial and art-based designs, the Mobile Dwelling Unit (MDU) is a shipping container-based proposal. The MDU is a prototype mobile home for the growing number of people who prefer (or whose job requires them) to move around the world on a regular basis. Although it utilises a standard shipping container for its basic structure it requires extensive modifications to function properly as a comfortable home. The result is a self-contained compact house, with push-out sections for sleeping, bathroom, kitchen, and storage facilities that, because of the standard size and form of the container, fit into existing transportation infrastructure. The MDU is designed to be located at any of the world's ports, transported on ISO truck beds and container ships, and slotted into a specially made service support frame at its destination. It allows the owners to have a home in every port, a real dedicated and personal dwelling with the continuity of their own possessions, though with a changing view from the window. Though the idea of a flexible, infrastructure-based, ever-changing city environment is by no means new (Buckminster Fuller and Archigram proposed it – Kisho Kurokawa and Richard Rogers tried to build it) this idea makes use of readily available, well-tested logistical systems that genuinely support the relocation of dwellings on a continuous basis rather than the appearance of plug-in architecture without the reality.

The prototype was constructed in 2003 for the Walker Art Center and the Art Museum of the University of Santa Barbara and has since been transported across the USA from west to east and north to south. The container needed extensive strengthening to take on its new role, not because of the weight of the added components but because the strength of the base structure stems from its unitary construction – perforating the skin weakens this. Internal fittings are standard household appliances built into a practical plywood, galvanised metal, and plastic aesthetic. The push-out elements are simply operated by hand – sealing in the open and closed position is by a rubber gasket at the joining of the moving and fixed element. Two things are remarkable about the realisation of the design: because the 'working' elements of home, kitchen, bathroom, storage, entertainment, are pushed out from the central space, the main central area feels remarkably open and unrestricted; and for the same

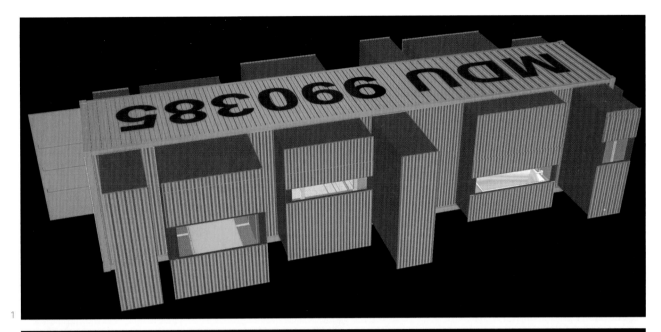

1/2   Computer generated images of the
Mobile Dwelling Unit (MDU) and its potential
deployment in a vertical frame stack.

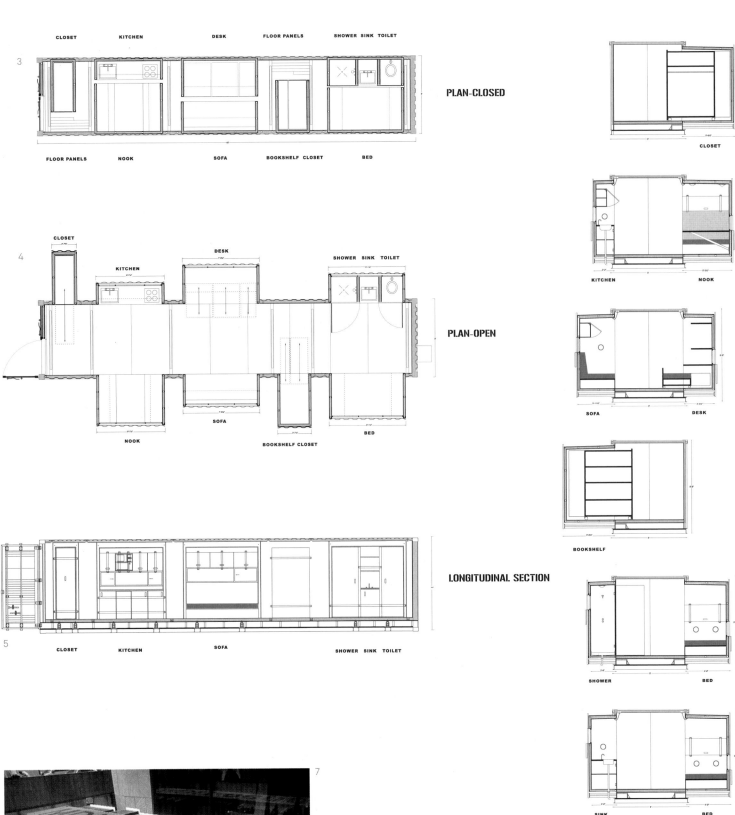

PLAN-CLOSED

PLAN-OPEN

LONGITUDINAL SECTION

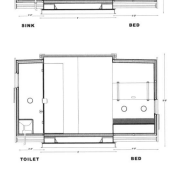

3–6 Plans and sections of the MDU.
7 On site at the Whitney Museum,
Manhattan, New York, USA.
8 Interior of the MDU in deployed mode.

8

reason it feels very interactive, a house that can be manipulated and changed rather than being fixed in layout.
When closed up the MDU is anonymous and like any other
mobile container, protecting its contents – when open the
personality of the home is on view as the residents push
and pull the parts they are using into operation.

The seemingly inevitable development of the MDU
is the prototype Container Home Kit (CHK), which LOT-EK
has developed as a commercially viable, affordable housing system. More than 20 million containers lie unused
in Western ports as the imbalance in the global economy
means that after shipping goods to market in Europe
and North America, few are returned. Recycling these
containers on a large scale could have significant sustain-
ability impact. Once again, the CHK is therefore built
from standard ISO shipping containers, though this time
using a modular system to build houses using two to eight
containers and ranging from 60 square metres to 240
square metres. Shifting the arrangement of the containers
provides covered porches and first floor terraces and
further containers can be utilised to make a car port, tool
shed, and even a swimming pool. Standard materials are

used to fit out the containers with insulation, wall-board-
ing, doors and windows, plumbing, and electrical supply,
however, the powerful industrial image remains a large
part of the concept's character. Transportation of the
factory-fitted units is carried out on standard truck beds
with the CHK units fitted with internal props to prevent
damage due to flexing of the frame. LOT-EK's CHK design
is one of a range of buildings created by an international
consortium of designers and manufacturers based around
the world, who offer up the possibility of prefabricated
portable dwellings built from recycled components in a
contemporary manner.

9

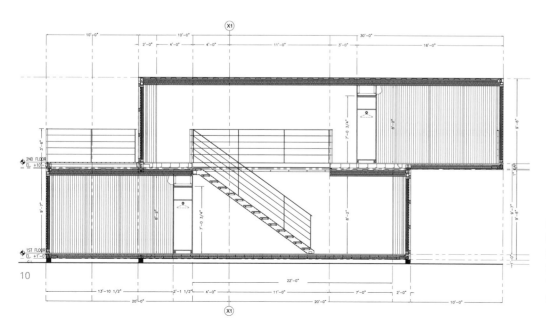

10

9/10 Computer generated image of the
Container Home Kit (CHK) six module unit
(plus an additional one for the swimming
pool). Longitudinal section through the CHK.
11 Plans, sections and elevations of the
six module CHK.

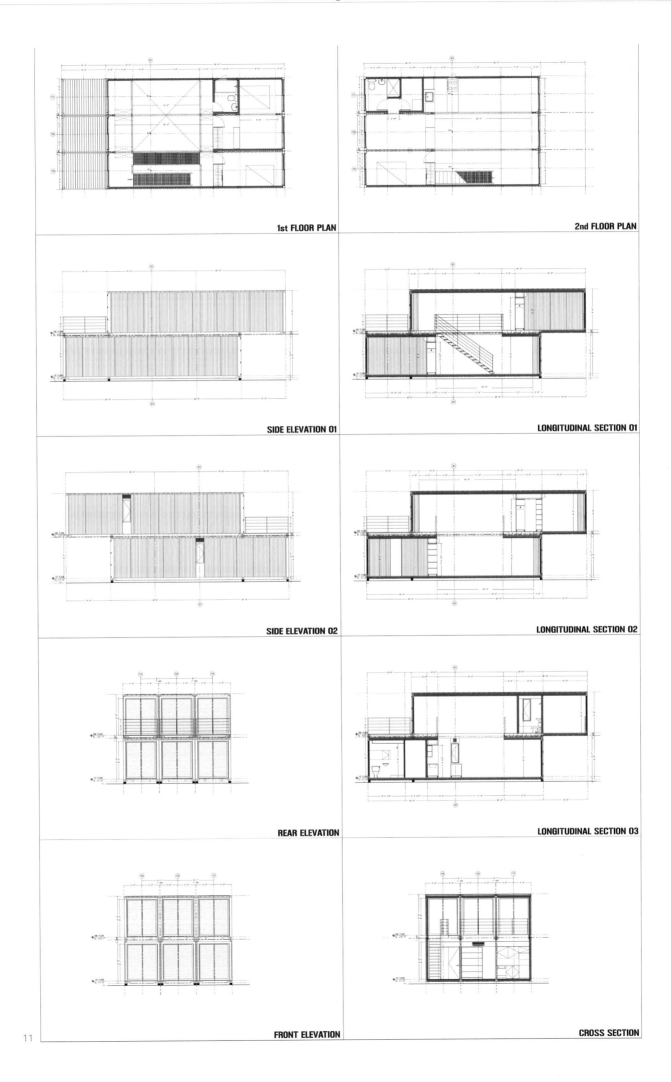

1st FLOOR PLAN

2nd FLOOR PLAN

SIDE ELEVATION 01

LONGITUDINAL SECTION 01

SIDE ELEVATION 02

LONGITUDINAL SECTION 02

REAR ELEVATION

LONGITUDINAL SECTION 03

FRONT ELEVATION

CROSS SECTION

Public Art Lab
Mobile Museums

2004 (Mobile Studios, 2006)
Architects: Hans J. Wiegner with Gruber + Popp
Architekten, Berlin, Germany
Concept and idea: Public Art Lab; Susa Pop (project
management), Ela Kagel (multimedia concept),
David Farine (IT infrastructure)
Client: Public Art Lab

Perhaps the most important (yet most difficult to evaluate) feature of portable architecture is the reaction that it creates in those who experience it. Practical benefits are relatively easy to understand once they are quantified, however, the way in which people respond to the temporary characteristics of structures they are accustomed to thinking of as permanent is complex. Portable buildings can do almost anything that permanent ones can and they are also frequently capable of fulfilling other functions that would be impossible by any other means. Portable buildings have a low environmental impact; they may be located in rural or urban situations with minimal long-term effects. They can make use of a temporary identifiable address that is of value to both the operator and the visitor in that high-profile locations can be used to increase the numbers of people reached in a given time period. Unusual building forms that are temporarily sited in familiar settings can also change people's view of their environment and give some the impetus to appreciate its positive and negative attributes more clearly.

Artists' work that crosses the boundaries between installation and architecture has an important role to play in bringing a new and different appreciation of familiar places and environments. Joep van Lieshout is a Dutch environmental and performance artist who has created a wide range of provocative work from his studio outside Rotterdam which deals with the ability of personally manufactured objects to support our desire for personal freedom. In particular, his group of collaborators and assistants have manufactured a series of 'mobile homes' that are simultaneously sensuous, romantic, amusing, and, at least to a certain degree, practical proposals for transportable, towable, and clip-on living and sleeping spaces. Another example is British artist Simon Blackmore's Sprite Musketeer. It is a standard touring caravan commercially built in the 1970s that has been converted into a mobile contemporary art space. This project explores the characteristics of place by locating it at critical positions alongside the road in such a way that visitors sit inside and admire a framed view of the landscape that alludes to those painted in previous generations by great artists such as J.M.W. Turner.

The Mobile Museums project is based on the idea of a completely accessible museum that, instead of

1

1 Mobile Museums deployed in Barcelona,
Spain, 2004.

containing all the art and exhibiting it to visitors in one
central location, has numerous exhibits in small buildings
that travel from place to place. It was inspired by the
vision of famous American minimalist artist Mark Rothko
who described a number of small museums, each devoted
to one artist, which the visitor could enter and then be
alone with the work for an hour. Public Art Lab is an inter-
disciplinary arts agency based in Berlin. Working with
artist Hans Wiegner, artist and arts manager Susa Pop
developed the idea for small mobile museums that could
be inhabited, used, and interpreted by different artists.
Architects Gruber and Popp supplied technical expertise
on construction and mobility. The ambition was to create
a new sort of museum that would temporarily occupy
important public spaces in the centre of cities. Even
though the actual buildings were modest in size, they
would have the capacity to metamorphose the spaces that
they occupied, giving them a new purpose and identity,
albeit transitory.

The theme for the buildings, though varied by the
artist's interpretation, was a luminous white cubic object.
The buildings were designed to be both intriguing and

anonymous – to contribute interest to the public spaces
they inhabited but also to be sufficiently neutral to allow
the artists' work to be predominant. The mobility of the
buildings not only meant they could be moved from place
to place but also that they could be relocated in different
juxtapositions creating a unique mobile community
in each place. Beginning in Potsdamer Platz, Berlin, the
museums travelled around Europe including Vienna
and Barcelona.

Each artist was given a construction kit consisting
of modular, recycled PVC sheets, which they could assemble into a unique structure measuring a maximum of
10 square metres. The constructional concept had to be
robust but also easy to assemble and dismantle for
transportation. The floors have a substantial wooden
frame that enables movement via forklift truck. The walls
are made from double skin PVC rigid-foam sheets. The
ceilings are wooden frames clad in PVC and serve to brace
the structure. The parts of each structure are sized to
fit onto a standard flat-bed truck no bigger than 2.4 metres
wide and 3.1 metres high. This simple, tough construction
managed to withstand many relocations between sites,

2–4 Mobile Museums Mobile Studios
project, 2006.
5/6 Mobile Museums in Berlin, 2004.
7 Section through structure.

5

6

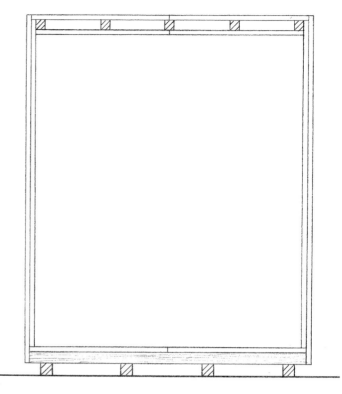

7

the artists' performances and installations, and the hundreds of visitors who passed through the buildings. Artists could create a completely enclosed space to generate a personally determined internal character into which the public entered, or an open pavilion that formed a focus for performance or installation.

In a project that anticipated the next phase of the Mobile Museums project, the artist Caroline von Grone used the structure as a publicly accessible studio in which she invited visitors to become models and thereby participants in as well as observers of the artistic process. In 2006, the Mobile Museums were rebuilt to accommodate the Mobile Studios consisting of the Editorial, Live, and Talk Studio. These formed the basis that different groups could use and adapt at each of the locations they visited including Belgrade, Bratislava, Sofia, and Gdansk where a mobile webcast studio was added to provide virtual documentation of the event. The Editorial Studio was the largest at 12 square metres. It contained a 4 metre long work surface and four workstations with live internet connections, scanners, and streaming servers – here content was distributed to television, radio, press, and the internet. The Live Studio was an empty white space put at the disposal of artists for a 24 hour period to create their own performances and installations. The Talk Studio was used to host discussions and interviews in the host city with space for four participants and two digital cameras.

Gollifer Langston Architects

Classroom of the Future

2007
Architect: Gollifer Langston Architects, London, UK;
Andy Gollifer and Mark Langston
Consultants: Michael Hadi Associates (engineers);
Arup (building services engineers); J. S. Fraser
(specialist coach builders); Measur (cost consultants)
Client: Camden Education Authority

The Classroom of the Future initiative was set up by the UK government's Department for Education and Skills (DfES) to challenge current thinking about education buildings. With over £5 billion spent annually in the UK on school facilities it is essential that it is spent wisely, and the initiative was created not only to promote new design ideas but also to prototype them and test them with full-size implementation. One of the key factors that was identified as driving new school design was the implementation of innovation in ICT (information and communication technology). Retrofitting old schools with new state-of-the-art facilities in this area is not only extremely costly but also restricts its use to the children from that school. Camden Education Authority in London therefore commissioned a mobile classroom that could move around its area delivering the highest quality facilities to all its children. This meant that the equipment would be used extremely intensively by a large number of pupils. It also meant that they would have an event-filled teaching experience benefiting from the novelty value bestowed by the building's ephemeral nature.

Architect Mark Langston wanted to create a classroom that was physically and metaphorically a vehicle for learning – its great difference from the normal school buildings being used as a method to generate children's excitement and interest. However, there were many practical considerations too; the building would have to be easy to transport, in use quickly and efficiently, comfortable, and sustainable in energy use. It also had to be able to adapt to future changes in equipment, teaching, and deployment scenarios. The concept was therefore to create a building that would be transported on the back of a standard articulated lorry 2.5 metres wide by 9 metres long – the fact that the building would stay in each location for a whole school term (twelve weeks) meant it was uneconomic to build in its own travelling chassis. The classroom would operate with a group of 15 students at a time working on cross-curriculum projects including a wide range of complex media tasks including digital film editing and music production. It was to contain eight IT workstations, a 2.1 metre LCD screen for group teaching, and its own server and environmental plant.

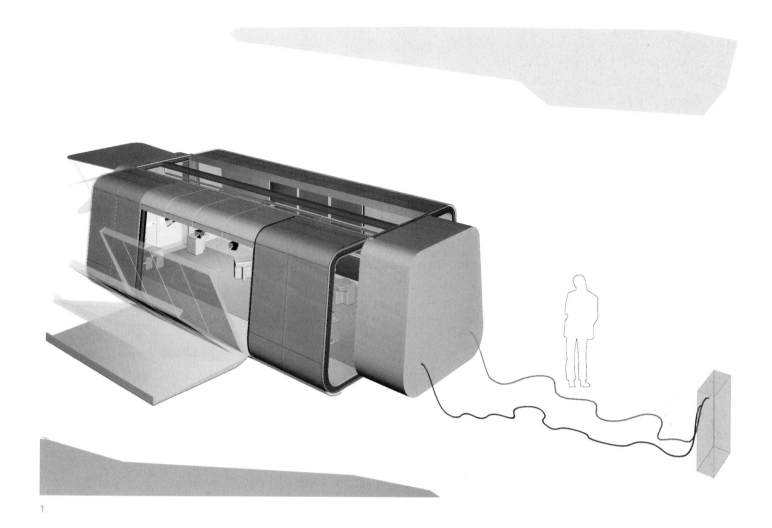

1

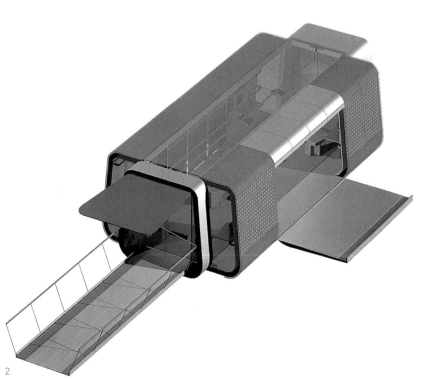

2

1/2 Classroom of the Future – computer generated images.

3

4

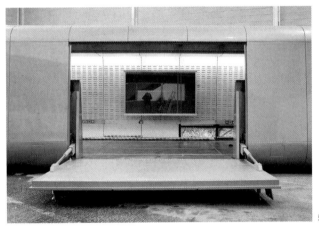

5

3–5   The classroom's first deployment,
London, UK, 2007.
6–8   Plan, longitudinal, and cross section.

Clearly the manufacture of such a building would have as much to do with vehicles as it would with architecture and so specialist coach building firm J.S. Fraser were appointed as constructors. However, they were also an important part of the development team with their experience in building mobile facilities such as the extensive hospitality suites used by Formula One racing teams at Grand Prix circuits around the world. Project leader Greg Field worked in close collaboration with the architects and engineers to develop the project, sharing information and combining expertise in order to reach the best solution. The design process involved much more prototyping than is normal because this was a standard procedure for Fraser.

Construction began with the sourcing of a standard steel chassis on which to build up the superstructure. Steel was selected for this because of its strength but also to maximise internal space in what would have to be a compact form in order to be easily transportable. The cladding is powder-coated aluminium sheeting insulated with a special honeycomb aluminium product, Actis MultiPro TS250, which is used in the aerospace industries. Though the exterior is all shiny metal, the interior is per-

forated birch ply panels. The air-conditioning is a maritime unit made by Crusair, used primarily for luxury yachts. Although the classroom usually plugs into power and communications connections at its host school, it also has its own back-up batteries boosted by a commercially available photovoltaic panel and a 0.5 metre wind turbine mounted on a 6 metre high deployable mast. The power generated is displayed inside the classroom.

The classroom is transported in its closed configuration. When it arrives on site, hydraulic legs are deployed from concealed panels at each end – these drop down and then raise the facility up above the bed of the lorry, which then drives out. The legs retract and lower the building to the ground. The facility is then connected to external power – typically schools will have a conduit running into the siting area ready for mobile classrooms and other facilities. The hydraulic legs are retracted behind their concealing panels and the system is then used to push out the sides of the building to increase its internal width by 1.5 metres. These expanding panels have glazed sections to admit natural light. The entrance is at one end of the building – a canopy is manually

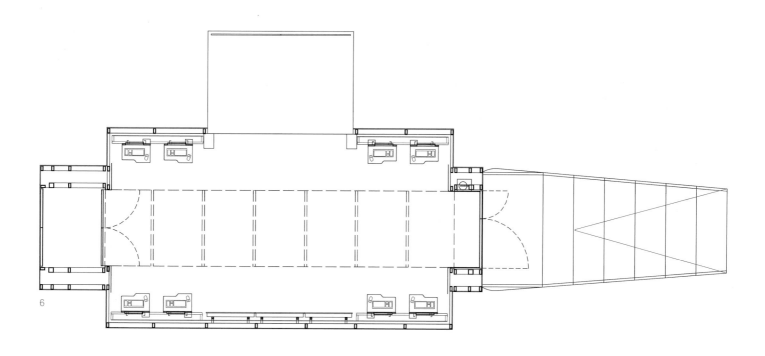

6

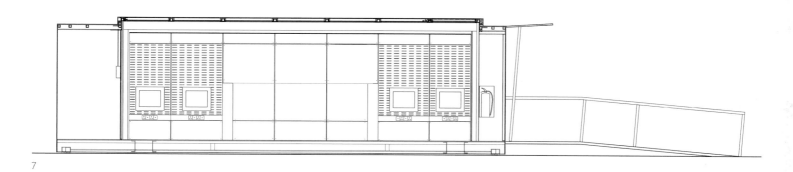

7

unfolded and an entrance ramp and handrails are
assembled from components carried within the facility.
The classroom is normally used in this configuration,
however, to involve more students, one of the sides can
be fully folded down by hydraulics to provide a perform-
ance/presentation set-up with additional external
built-in sound and lighting systems. A double glazed
rooflight manufactured in Canada by Vision Control
(Unicel Architectural) contains motorised solar control
louvres that also allow the interior to be blacked out for
visual presentations.

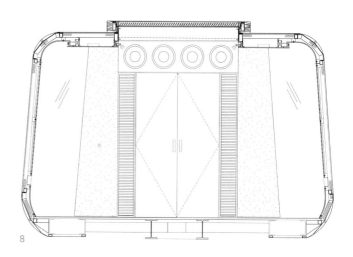

8

Theo Jansen
Animaris Rhinoceros Transport

2004
Artist/Designer: Theo Jansen, Ypenburg,
The Netherlands
Consultant: Heijmerink en Wagenmakers,
Nieuwgein (steelwork)
Client: Geuzenveld/Slotermeer Town Council

Art is not architecture – but in certain cases and situations art and architecture have similar goals and similar effects. Environmental sculpture has many common factors with the world of building: it must have a site and technological input in its construction, and it shares considerations about health and safety, maintenance, and cost. This is in addition to the formal aesthetic comparisons between appearance and meaning that any visual design discipline must engage with. Architecture that is mobile has the same design considerations as its static counterpart – sculpture that is mobile can be compared in the same way.

Theo Jansen is an artist working in the field of mobile sculpture. Since 1980 he has developed an evolutionary series of sculptures that have explored the concept of animated mobile form. Jansen initially studied physics at university and has retained his interest in science and mechanics, writing computer programmes that created artificial 'life'. This led to the development of a computer model for a quadruped 'life' form. His interest is now applied in an innately practical way in delivering to his sculptures the capacity to move.

In 1990, Jansen wrote an article speculating about the creation of a mechanical animal called a *Strandloper* (beach walker or roller) and soon after he began to build his first real version, giving himself just one year to explore its potential. For this first project Jansen bought some plastic electric conduit in a do-it-yourself store – this basic material is still a major component in many of his sculptures. He called his first sculpture *Animaris Vulgaris* and so began the theme of 'hereditary' mechanical beasts that grow and evolve through the artist's intervention. *Vulgaris'* physical form was 2 metres by 2 metres by 0.6 metres though its geometry was first evolved in computer and smaller-scale models. The fundamental premise of the *Strandbeest*, as Jansen has named his sculptures, is that they do not use the wheel but the foot to enable movement, rising and falling in a different position – the wheel is a machine element whilst the leg is natural. In 1992 he built *Animaris Currens*, which moved with the aid of a crankshaft and introduced heat formed joints to strengthen the structure. A year later he made *Animaris Sabulosa*, the first of the building-size sculptures at 8 metres by 2 metres by 2 metres. *Sabulosa* means sand –

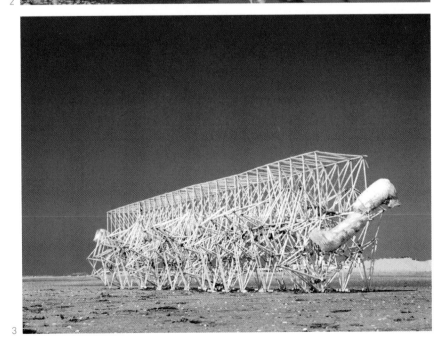

1 *Animaris Sabulosa.*
2 *Excelsus Groot.*
3 *Geneticus.*

4

5

4 *Animaris Percipiere.*
5 *Animaris Currens Ventosa.*
6 *Rhinoceros Transport.*
7–10 Construction details.

6

7   8   9   10

the sculpture was so named because it gathered sand in its tail. Similarly, *Animaris Ventosa* (walks on winds) earned its name because it could move by the power of the wind. Jansen attaches stories to the creation of each sculpture to stir the imagination and belief in the creation of these new forms of 'life' but also simply because it is amusing for the artist and those who engage with his art.

The *Animaris* use short lengths of tubes because they distort and lose strength if they are too long. Jansen developed a simple machine to help make the sculpture components, which enables accurate angles to be formed when the tubes are bent and strong joints to be formed by heat welding. Since 2001 he has also been developing powered sculptures that move under air pressure. The main trouble has been in creating simple but effective pistons that are sufficiently airtight to make a pneumatic pump that is strong enough to move a large object. Typically, Jansen uses disposable plastic drinks bottles as compressed air reservoirs. Standard neoprene and silicone seals and gaskets are used to make the pneumatic system operational.

The largest sculpture built to date is the *Animaris Rhinoceros Transport*, which stands 4.7 metres tall and is capable of carrying three children inside its muddy skin. The *Rhinoceros* is unusual in that it was a commission from the town of Geuzenveld/Slotermeer with funding from Art Amsterdam, but also in that Jansen did not build it on his own. Because of its size, the sculpture was built with a steel skeleton covered by a polyester skin finished with a painted 'mud' surface that gives it the impression of great solidity. Despite its total weight of 3.2 tonnes, the structure is easy to move by people pulling on a rope or even on its own by the wind. It is large, bulky and yet also animated – contrasting imagery that reinforces Jansen's imposed animalistic identity. It is the size of a building but is designed to move with comparatively little external effort, definitely without mechanical motive power, which would undermine its 'beast-like' character. The *Strandbeest* are art objects that question the relationship between architectural-sized objects and animals by investing construction with mobility.

Tadao Ando Architect and Associates

Karaza Theatre

1987–1988
Architect: Tadao Ando Architect and Associates, Osaka, Japan; Tadao Ando
Client: Kara Juro and Seiyo Corporation
Location: Sendai and Tokyo, Japan

Tadao Ando is perhaps the most celebrated architect from the second generation of Japanese post-war designers whose work has followed on from those like Kisho Kurokawa who were the first to establish a definitive modern aesthetic in the 1970s. The early work with which he gained his reputation consists of precisely controlled houses that synthesise an international style modernism with a more spiritual Eastern sensibility. Tradition still plays a defining role in contemporary Japanese architecture and even though his buildings are generally constructed of concrete, steel, and glass, Ando still refers to the skill of the master carpenter in the permanent impression of the carefully crafted temporary timber shuttering used in their construction. In 1985, Ando designed the Karaza Theatre, a seminal mobile arts building that fuses the traditional aspects of Japanese building with contemporary strategies and technologies.

The building was designed for the travelling avant garde theatre/performance company led by Kara Juro who up to that time had used a red tent for their events. Despite the innovative nature of Juro's work, tradition also plays a part. The company used a stage area that consisted of a small raised platform divided by a symbolic river, a stylised version of the performance set used for traditional Japanese comic and tragic theatre. The original concept for the Karaza building was for a wooden structure with the image and form of a watchtower that would be sited at Asakusa in Tokyo. The building would be constructed entirely of timber, which Ando describes as an 'eternal' material. This may seem paradoxical to Westerners as it can be destroyed much more easily than other materials such as stone, however, as timber is a natural growing product, this perception relates to its constant renewal.

When the brief was changed to the idea of a moving building, the form remained but the main structure was altered to a system that could be erected and dismantled easily. Rather than design a dedicated system with the resultant dramatic increase in budget, Ando utilised scaffolding. By faxing a set of comprehensive instructions the building process could be carried out by local labour in advance of the theatre company stage team's arrival on site. Ando's early sketches of the building show it erected in dramatic locations such as the harbour front in New York, reminiscent of Aldo Rossi's 1979 *Teatro del Mondo*,

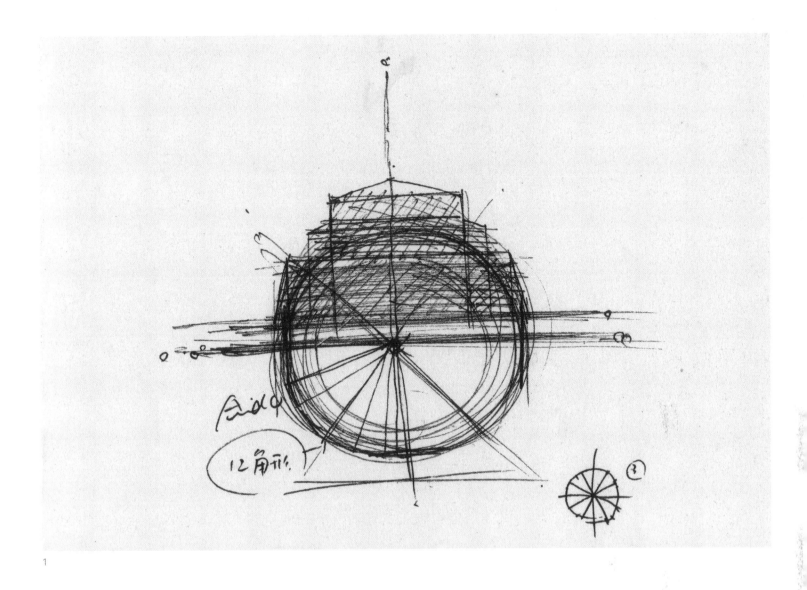

1

1 Karaza Theatre sketch design.
2 External view showing the tension membrane roof and boarded cladding.

2

3

4

a transportable theatre built on a barge and floated from city to city along the Mediterranean coast.

The building's form is a multi-layered dodecahedron in plan, intended to represent the cosmos. The walls are made from black stained wooden boards, which have gaps between them on the lower outer wall and are solid for the theatre walls. Simple bleacher seating covered with carpet is used for the 600 seats in the auditorium. A staircase rises between the two outer walls, following the profile of the building and leading to the elevated main entrance. The main approach to this is via a *taikobashi*, an arched bridge, which symbolises the passage from the world of reality to the world of illusion and from the present world to the *higan*, a Buddhist description of the world after death. Built around the entire complex is a traditional fence of woven bamboo called a *takeyarai* used to emphasise the other-worldly nature of a space used for theatre. All these symbolic elements contribute to the significance of the building for visitors, who are aware of these traditional meanings from the representational elements commonly found in house and temple architecture. Their application to a contemporary building in no way dilutes this power.

The main building components, scaffolding, timber boarding, and bleacher seating, are all made from locally available standard items, though a number of special elements were also transported between sites. The roof was a red-coloured tension membrane, reminiscent of the Juro group's previous transportable shelter, the red tent. This was fixed to a very light steel truss, 27 metres high, which spanned the 18 metre wide auditorium space. Rods that firmly braced the inner and outer walls 4 metres apart and another red membrane roof that covered this space were also part of the transported component package. The constructional procedure consisted of laying out the geometry of the building on the ground then erecting the scaffolding with the use of two mobile cranes. One mobile crane was located in the centre of the space and the building form was built around it with a small gap to allow it to leave when the building reached full height. The timber cladding, stairs, and roof membrane were added after the scaffolding structure was complete. Erection took 15 days. The building was first erected in the Northern Honshu city of Sendai in 1987.

5

6

3/4 Entrance bridge and route around inside
the external wall of the building.
5/6 Karaza Theatre interior – carpet covered
bleacher type seating. The dark fabric
covered panels conceal access gangways
and production.

The Karaza Theatre was not the only temporary building designed by Ando. In 1990, he built another theatre for photographer Bishin Jumonji and in 1992 he designed the Japanese pavilion at Expo 92 in Seville, Spain, which was one of the most imposing buildings on the entire site. Conforming to the Japanese design philosophy based on *kinari*, unadorned beauty, the hardwood-clad building was based on a series of grand timber columns that culminated in a constructed capital similar to that found in ancient temples though built to a simpler pattern on a much larger scale. The message that its form conveyed was of a present-day object based on a valued history.

The Karaza Theatre and the Japanese Pavilion utilised contemporary architectural principles and technology, but because their use was harmonised with cultural and social concepts familiar to the society that they served, they may be seen as landmarks in the continuum of ideas that establish the basis of architectural form in general. That these traditional concepts have found new relevance for contemporary functions proves that the transference of spiritual ideas about architecture can be expressed in new building techniques. The practical benefits of using more advanced constructional methods and new logistical approaches in the provision of buildings are more easily accepted as a beneficial innovation when associated with a continuing social and spiritual understanding.

7–9 Erection process. The site set out
with delivery of scaffolding underway.
10–11 Typical site layout and
plan/elevation.

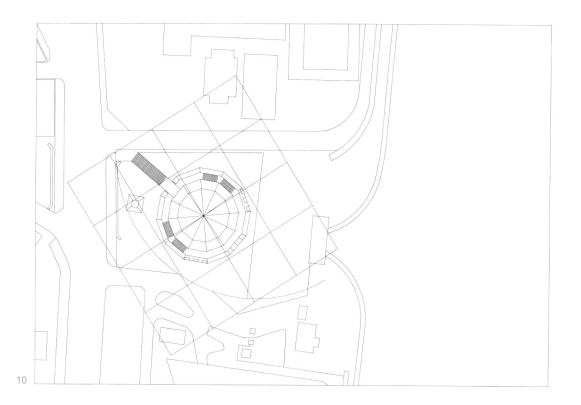

10

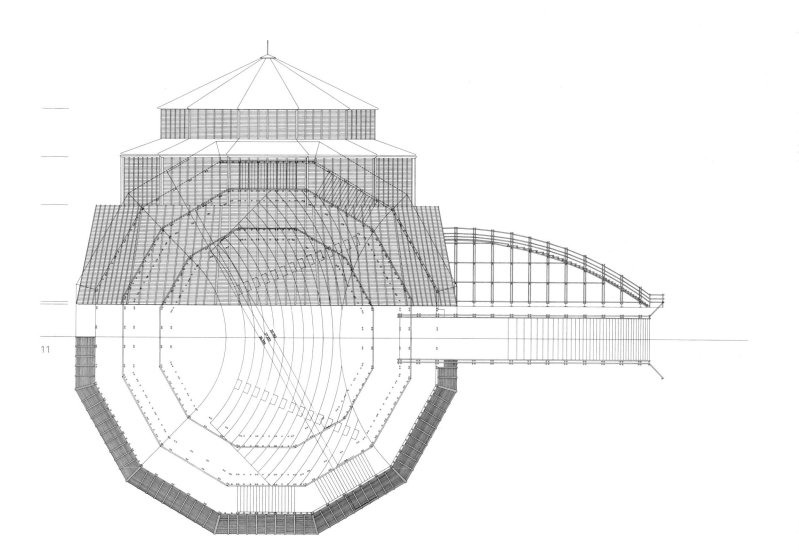

11

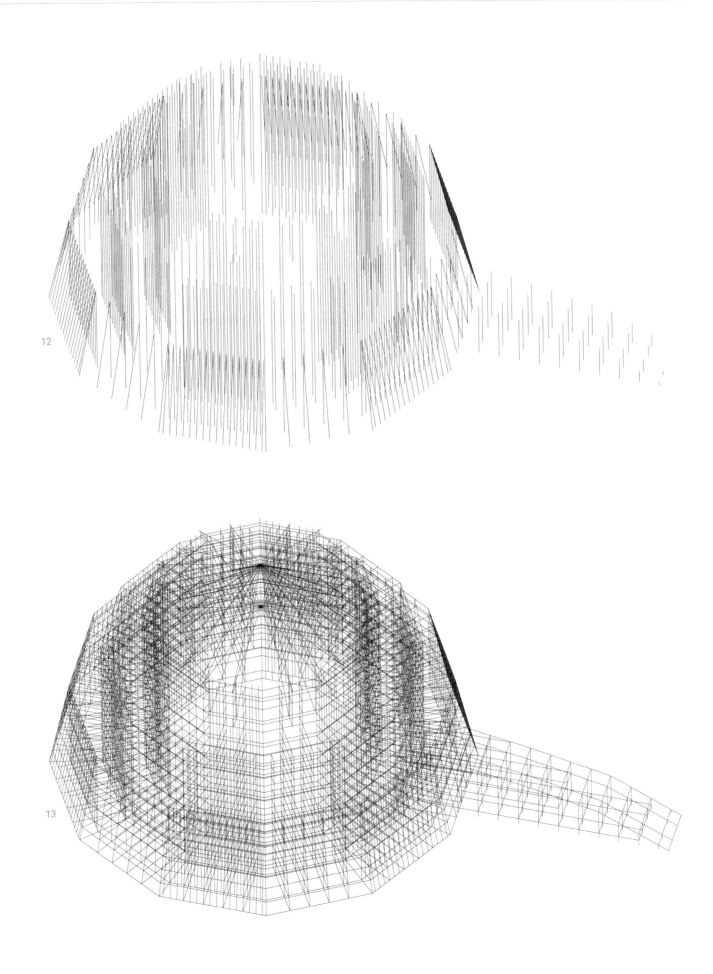

12

13

12/13 CAD drawings showing the
erection process.
14/15 Constructional details.
Roof structure. Scaffolding bracing.

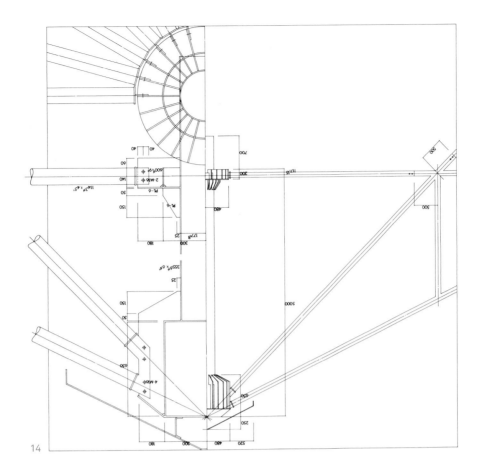

14

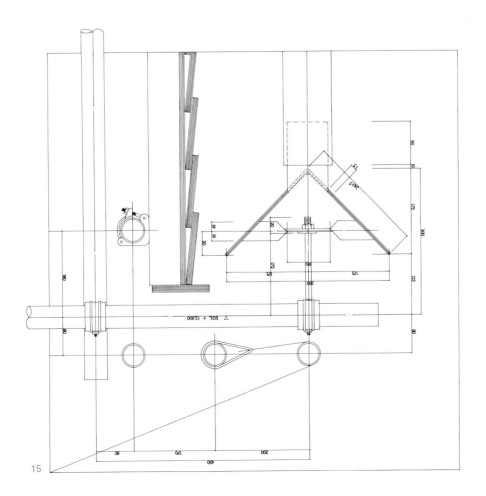

15

NASA
ISS TransHAB

1997–2000

Architect: Advanced Development Office, NASA, JSC,
Lead space architect: Kriss J. Kennedy, Houston, USA
Engineer: Advanced Programs Office, NASA,
JSC, Structures and Mechanics Division: Dr. William
Schneider, Horacio de la Fuente, Gregg Edeen,
Jasen Raboin.
Consultants: ILC Dover Inc.
Client: Exploration Office/Advanced Development
Office NASA, Johnson Space Center (JSC)

Building for temporary deployment on a remote site has different design parameters to building permanent long-term structures. In portable building, the advantages of a holistic approach to design and construction can be easily understood. To build conventionally in a remote location is in many cases impossible. Components and materials transportation must be carefully considered and all construction must be carried out by a dedicated on-site team whose shelter and provisions must also be provided. Foresight and planning are essential as mistakes and omissions in the design are far less easily solved when the design team, component manufacturer, and materials supplier are at a great distance. If the building has also to be erected in extreme conditions or is required to be in use quickly, the advantages of integrated design and construction become more relevant. The building may also have to be capable of re-erection at other sites for logistical or economic reasons in which case this streamlined, efficient construction process becomes an essential rather than a desirable characteristic of a successful project.

Though the extreme environments of the Arctic and Antarctica have been used as models for extraterrestrial situations, and there are parallels between vehicles designed for space travel and the bottom of the oceans, conditions in space are more extreme than anywhere found on the surface of this planet. Despite this, the logistical problems of building in space have many similarities with Earth-bound temporary building design. Virtually all the components for the construction and transportation of extraterrestrial buildings must be manufactured using technology that is based on experience drawn from Earth-bound projects. These pre-manufactured sub-assemblies must then be transported many thousands of miles to their deployment location. There are also great limitations on their weight and size because of the payload problems associated with lifting any object free of the Earth's gravity, and they must therefore not only be able to resist the harshest environment yet encountered, but also be as lightweight and compact in transportation as possible. Despite the remoteness and unusual nature of their site and the unique operations associated with their special purpose, space exploration shelters will still have to support the many pragmatic human activities that are required for a similar expedition

1

1 Computer generated image of
the ISS TransHAB deployed as part
of the International Space Station.

on Earth. The design of portable buildings for Earth and extraterrestrial use therefore has many similarities in that it relates to directly comparable functions, materials technology, manufacturing techniques, transportation, and deployment strategies.

Beyond the current ongoing expansion of the International Space Station, the next stage in manned space exploration is focused on a return to the Moon and the establishment of an outpost. It is the planet about which we know most and it has therefore been possible to determine the tasks that would take place on the planet's surface and select possible habitation sites. The lunar habitat project has been developed primarily by space architect Kriss Kennedy, a graduate of the University of Houston, Sasakawa International Center for Space Architecture (SICSA), USA, who originally trained as an architect, indeed the design process for this project has many parallels with conventional building design involving a team working under a lead designer, consultant engineers, client representatives, and manufacturers. Many of the tasks associated with a lunar settlement can be compared to the establishment of a remote outpost on Earth.

In the same way that a terrestrial building cannot be erected without support facilities for building personnel, administration, storage of materials, and specialist workshops, a lunar habitation outpost requires support infrastructure that is available instantly on arrival at the building site. This must provide safe shelter for humans and machines whilst the main facilities are being erected. In a dangerous, airless environment it is also important to keep external operations to a minimum. This significantly affects construction logistics in that all procedures need to be carefully rehearsed before the mission. Once on site, a combination of crew and robotic assembly should, as far as possible, be carried out in safe environments.

As the habitat will be so remote, other non-habitation structures are required that are just as important for the operation of the outpost and the safety of the personnel as the habitation module. A permanent base will consist of a range of integrated facilities including a landing site, oxygen manufacturing facility, and power plant. The site of the first lunar base might simply be a flat area free of obstacles, however, early improvements such as the levelling, grading, and sealing of the surface to reduce dust

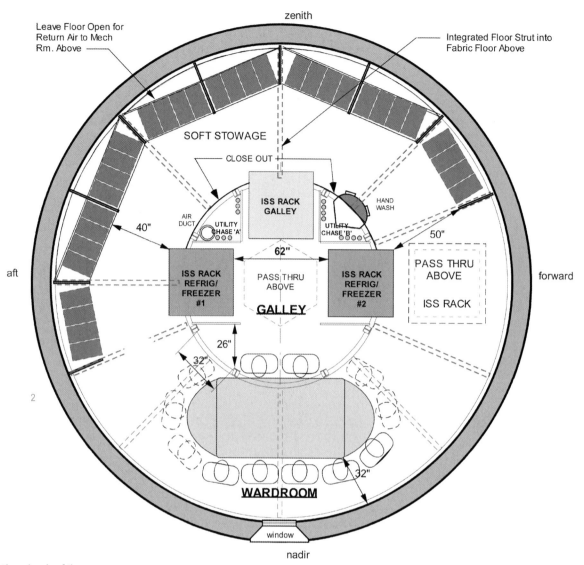

zenith

Leave Floor Open for
Return Air to Mech
Rm. Above

Integrated Floor Strut into
Fabric Floor Above

SOFT STOWAGE

CLOSE OUT

ISS RACK
GALLEY

HAND
WASH

AIR
DUCT

UTILITY
CHASE 'A'

UTILITY
CHASE 'B'

40"

50"

62"

aft

ISS RACK
REFRIG/
FREEZER
#1

PASS THRU
ABOVE

ISS RACK
REFRIG/
FREEZER
#2

PASS THRU
ABOVE

ISS RACK

forward

GALLEY

26"

32"

2

32"

WARDROOM

window

nadir

2–4 Plans of the three levels of the
ISS TransHAB (level 1, 2, and 3).

raised during arrival and departure of spacecraft would need to be made and eventually servicing and refueling facilities would be required.

Power requirements for an early lunar base would be in the region of 100 kilowatts, which would supply the environmental control systems, laboratory experiments, and vehicles and equipment used in building, exploration, living, and working on the lunar surface. A likely system consists of a flexible, solar-powered photovoltaic mat that could be unrolled on arrival to lie flat on the surface. As solar power is not available at night the array must provide sufficient energy to charge batteries for night-time use – an area of about two thousand square metres would therefore be required. Fuel storage would be most efficiently carried out in fuel cells, which have about a tenth of the weight of batteries. They chemically combine oxygen and hydrogen to form water, which releases energy and stores it by converting the water back into its separate components using electrolysis.

An oxygen plant would also be required, most probably utilising a mining process that would crush the lunar regolith to release small amounts of ilmenite, an oxygen-

bearing material which when mixed with hot hydrogen produces water and other oxides. The water can then be split into oxygen and hydrogen, the former stored in liquid form for conversion to gas as required, and the latter recycled back into the process.

The mobile deployable space habitat that is closest to commissioning is NASA's Transit Habitat (TransHAB). This project originally began as a design for the pressurised component of a future Mars transit vehicle. The journey from Earth to Mars will take up to six months each way and it is essential that during this time the travellers have safe and conducive environments on board their spacecraft in which to rest and work. The physical and psychological demands of this journey will be more extreme than any previously attempted and the creation of relatively spacious comfortable living spaces is extremely important, however, the payload necessary to build such large volumes in space from conventional rigid technology would be enormous. The inflatable solution developed for TransHAB makes possible the creation of a relatively lightweight structure manufactured in optimum construction conditions on Earth. This can be transported in compact

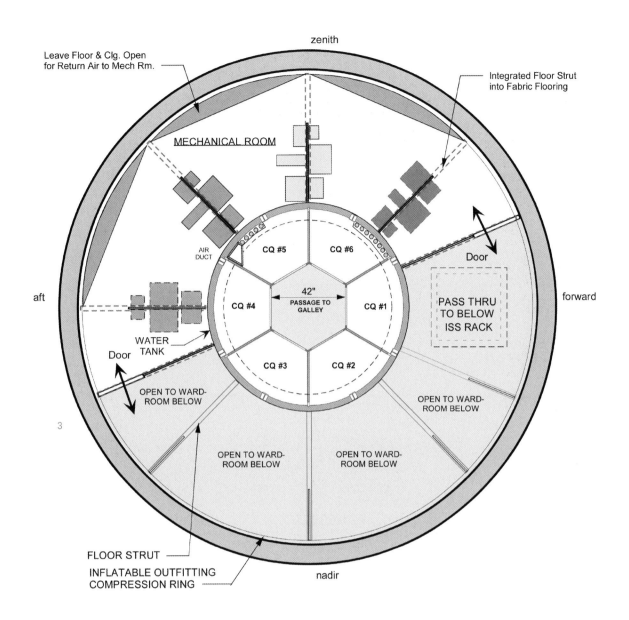

zenith

Leave Floor & Clg. Open
for Return Air to Mech Rm.

Integrated Floor Strut
into Fabric Flooring

MECHANICAL ROOM

AIR
DUCT

CQ #5   CQ #6

Door

aft

CQ #4

42"
PASSAGE TO
GALLEY

CQ #1

PASS THRU
TO BELOW
ISS RACK

forward

WATER
TANK

Door

CQ #3   CQ #2

OPEN TO WARD-
ROOM BELOW

OPEN TO WARD-
ROOM BELOW

3

OPEN TO WARD-
ROOM BELOW

OPEN TO WARD-
ROOM BELOW

FLOOR STRUT

INFLATABLE OUTFITTING
COMPRESSION RING

nadir

form in the payload bay of the Space Shuttle and then easily deployed with minimum assembly operations into a much bigger volume in space. It has also been designed so that it could be deployed on a remote planet's surface as part of a long-term base.

TransHAB is still a component of the future Mars mission, however, the increased emphasis on the International Space Station (ISS) has found it a new, more urgent alternative habitation module. The same characteristics that make the design an important part of the Mars mission would make it attractive for use as part of the ISS complex – in particular, at 12.19 metres long by 8.23 metres diameter it provides 342 cubic metres of pressurised volume, nearly three times the habitable space of a comparable standard ISS module. The habitat is divided into four 'floor' levels arranged around a central structural core. Three of the levels are living space – galley/wardroom and soft stowage on level 1, crew quarters and mechanical equipment room on level 2, crew health care/body cleansing and additional stowage on level 3. As well as a central passageway through the core, these three areas are linked by an 'atria' type space, providing a more open feel than would

normally be expected from the cramped confines of previous space vessel designs. The fourth level is a pressurised connecting tunnel to the rest of ISS. The habitat is designed to be capable of supporting the maximum ISS twelve-person crew, which occurs when the shuttle is docked for crew exchange – for example everyone can 'sit' together in the wardroom area. It also sleeps six, who each have their own private quarters with personal item storage, sleeping space, and entertainment/work station. This zone is also protected from excessive radiation during solar events by a water jacket. All the spaces are designed to utilise the standard rack systems that have been created for ISS – Full Body Cleansing Compartment (FBCC), Environmental Control and Life Support Systems (ECLSS), Crew Health Care Systems (CHeCS), communications, galley, refrigerator/freezer.

TransHAB's structure is a hybrid system that incorporates both inflatable and hard technologies to fulfill the peculiar, conflicting requirements of portability versus resistance to extreme environmental conditions. It thereby combines the safety and compatibility advantages of the rigid structure with the packaging and mass/volume

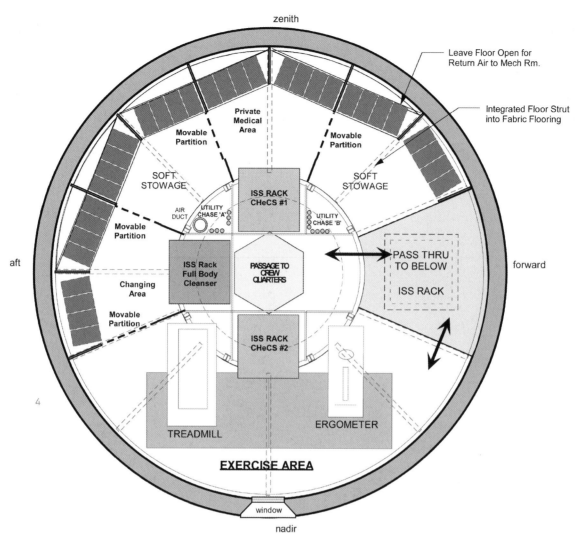

zenith

Leave Floor Open for
Return Air to Mech Rm.

Integrated Floor Strut
into Fabric Flooring

Private
Medical
Area

Movable
Partition

Movable
Partition

SOFT
STOWAGE

SOFT
STOWAGE

ISS RACK
CHeCS #1

AIR
DUCT

UTILITY
CHASE 'A'

UTILITY
CHASE 'B'

Movable
Partition

aft   forward

ISS Rack
Full Body
Cleanser

PASSAGE TO
CREW
QUARTERS

PASS THRU
TO BELOW

ISS RACK

Changing
Area

Movable
Partition

ISS RACK
CHeCS #2

4

TREADMILL

ERGOMETER

EXERCISE AREA

window

nadir

5 Computer generated cutaway images
of the ISS TransHAB.
6/7 Prototype undergoing testing at
the Johnson Space Center, Houston, USA.

efficiencies of the inflatable structure. The structural core consists of a hexagonal shaped tube made of composite longerons (columns) that connect to a tunnel unit at one end and a bulkhead at the other. These are braced by isogrid shelves which help the core resist the loads of launch but which can be repositioned after inflation to support floor beams and equipment. The inflatable shell is a multiple design consisting of four sets of layer systems each with its own function – the internal barrier and bladder, the structural restraint layer, the Micrometeoroid/orbital debris shield, and the thermal protection blanket. The inner layer of Nomex provides fire retardance and abrasion resistance – three plastic bladders form redundant air seals and four levels of Kevlar felt provide for evacuation of the shell between layers when the shell is packaged after testing prior to launch. The restraint layer is woven from 25 millimetre wide Kevlar straps specially developed to achieve more than 90% efficiency. The assembly is designed to contain four atmospheres of air pressure and each cylindrical strip has been tested to 12,500 pounds (5670 kilogrammes). The protection layer has to resist particle strikes at extremely high velocities.

The design philosophy is to incorporate a series of four Nextel ceramic fibre fabric layers, which absorb the energy and cause the particle to disintegrate as it moves through the successive barriers. A final backing layer of Kevlar provides the last line of resistance. This system has been found in testing to resist impacts by a 17 millimetre ball fired at 7 kilometres per second (25,105 kilometres per hour).

The TransHAB is transported into Earth orbit in the Shuttle's payload bay packaged within a lightweight Kevlar webbing container. Once the Shuttle docks with the ISS the TransHAB is removed from the bay and fixed to one of the station's modular nodes via the passageway at the end of the structural core. This will become the pressurised entry into the TransHAB. A similar unpressurised tunnel at the other end of the core contains the air inflation system for the outer shell, which maintains its operating pressure of 14.7 pounds per square inch. After inflation, the internal fabric floors can be deployed, the shelves positioned, equipment commissioned, and the habitat occupied.

The former Advanced Programs Office, Johnson Space Center, Houston, has made a full-scale prototype unit of

6

7

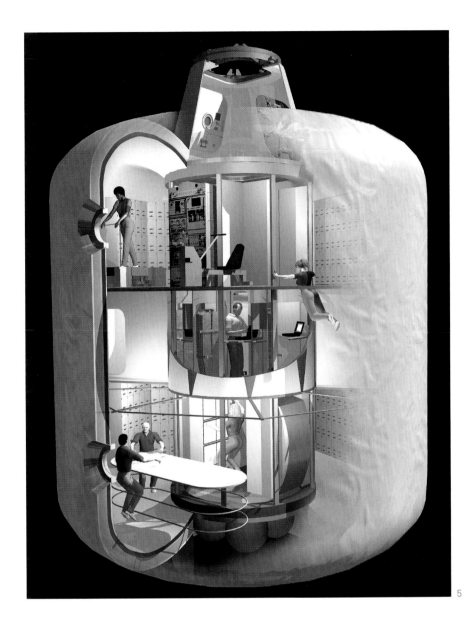

5

TransHAB in-house which has been inflated to operating pressure. The operational facility will also be made in-house though the central core will be made by Alenia, Italy, and the internal bladder made by ILC Dover Inc. The first module was intended for use as a safe living and working environment aboard ISS, but also for testing the effects on the crew of long-term space travel. Parts of the technology used in the development of TransHAB are already used in several US Defence Department scenarios such as high-performance rapid deployment shelters, but the construction strategies developed specifically for this project also have potential for use in other terrestrial situations, for example as a fuel tank, an underwater shelter, and as a divers' mobile hyperbaric decompression chamber.

The spin-offs that have resulted from technology developed for space exploration have been significant. Aluminium lithium, Vectran, Kevlar, and Nomex are new materials currently in use in the aerospace industry that can be transferred to more conventional situations. This phenomenon does not only apply to materials science but also to construction and assembly techniques – for example those that use automated systems and robotics.

Inflatable, enclosed-environment systems can be used in extreme and sensitive terrestrial sites such as the polar ice caps.

Research without direct precedent is an essential component of space research, but hardly present at all in the building industry in which there are many solutions available for a particular constructional issue, though none may be the best possible. Making use of innovative research from other areas is important, though it is sometimes difficult to recognise the benefits when the application is from a completely different sphere of design. Extraterrestrial habitation strategies can still be perceived as building construction, though they are undoubtedly highly specialised with circumstances of site and erection that could hardly be more different from those seen on Earth. Nevertheless, if they can be understood, there are sufficient similarities between the functional and constructional issues in both situations to allow techno-logy transfer to take place. The resultant benefits for construction technology in the building industry could be substantial.

Faber Maunsell
Halley VI

2004–2010
Designer: Faber Maunsell, Hertfortshire, UK;
Peter Ayres (project director), Michael Wright
(lead structural engineer), Neal Simmonds (services
engineer), Hugh Broughton Architects, London, UK;
Hugh Broughton
Consultants: DMJM H&N (cold climate and
remote relocation design): Bennett Associates
(mechanical legs design)
Client: British Antarctic Survey (BAS)

The British Antarctic Survey (BAS) undertakes a world-class programme of scientific research for the UK, and sustains an active and influential regional presence via a number of scientific stations located throughout the vast and desolate Antarctic region. The Halley station was established on the Brunt Ice Shelf in 1956 in preparation for the 1957/58 International Polar Year. The current facility is the fifth to be built there since that time, the previous four stations having succumbed to the relentless environmental conditions. Halley Research Station was where the hole in the ozone layer was first discovered in 1985.

Halley station is not situated on the ground but on a 150 metre thick floating ice shelf, which flows northward from the rock-based continent at a rate of 400 metres per year until it eventually breaks off into icebergs. Historical data has indicated that approximately every 50 to 60 years the Brunt Ice Shelf undergoes a calving event significantly reducing its size to a break-off point several kilometres 'in-land'. The existing station moves with the ice towards this inevitable break-off point and so it is necessary to plan ahead and create a new station before this happens. In 2004, a competition was launched to design a replacement station, which will be completed by 2010. The new building has to meet some of the most demanding environmental specifications ever created. The sun does not rise for three months during the Austral winter (although there is 24 hour daylight in mid-summer) and so the building must be able to withstand average external temperatures during this period of -30 degrees Celsius with an extreme limit of -56 degrees Celsius. In addition it must be able to cope with a site surface where there are rises due to snow accumulation of 1.5 metres each year. Another prime factor in the building's design was that it must have minimal impact on Antarctica's pristine environment as designated by the Antarctic Treaty Environmental Protocol. Remarkably, the Halley VI station must also be mobile. The ability to relocate the station is a necessity due to the unpredictability of the exact location of the break-off point and any subsequent consequences of that break-off that might result in a risk to the station or its operations. BAS requires the ability to tow the station out of danger at any point during the course of its design life.

The competition attracted 86 entries, six of which were short-listed, and from this group three design teams were

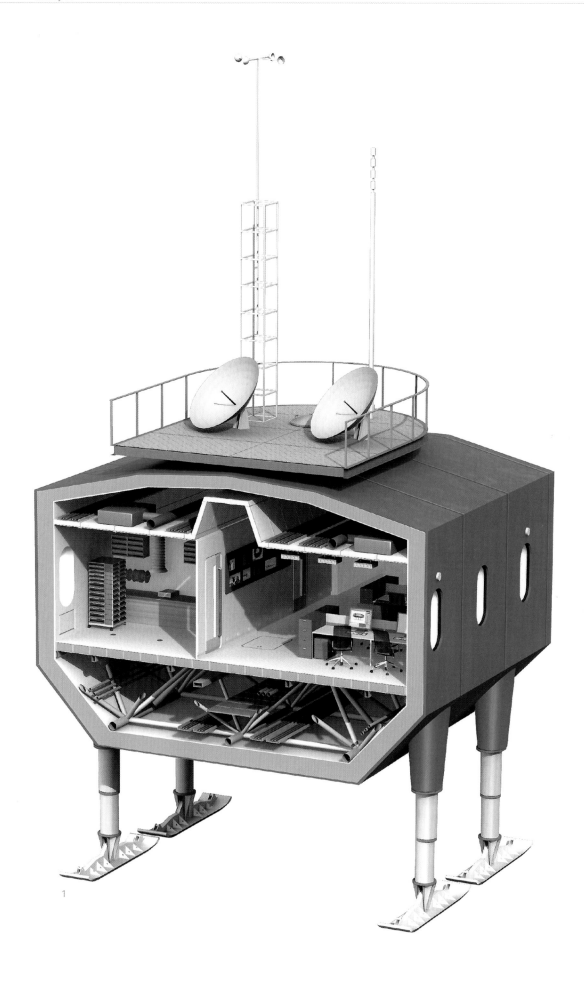

1 Computer generated cutaway image
through Halley VI science module.

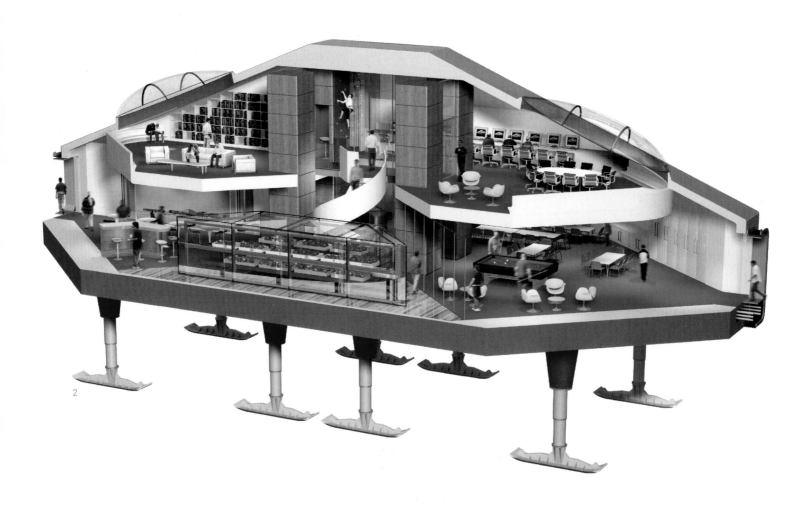

2

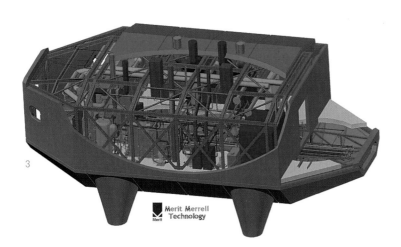

3

2 Computer generated cutaway image
through the central module.
3 Computer generated cutaway image
through the energy module.
4 Computer generated polar night view.

4

selected to visit the site. These three separate integrated teams then went on to develop more detailed proposals with BAS and contractor Morrison Falklands Ltd. In July 2005 the winning team for Halley VI was selected: Faber Maunsell working in partnership with Hugh Broughton Architects. Faber Maunsell are a firm of international engineers with experience in a wide range of civil, structural, and environmental engineering who have a proven track record in designing Antarctic facilities. The winning team's proposal was a direct response to the working and living demands of life in such an extreme climate, taking into account the comfort and security of residents, the flexibility necessary to allow a wide range of activities to take place within limited space, but also the importance of buildability and continuous operation in a place where a building failure can have disastrous rather than inconvenient consequences.

The station has a maximum capacity of 52 people in the summer with a permanent crew during the winter of 16. The design consists of a series of eight separate interconnected building modules that are supported at an elevated level on skis. The modular strategy allows for additional

buildings to be added if required but also for interchangeability of fittings and components. The skis provide foundations to the modules and enable them to be easily relocated or rearranged if operational requirements change. The central module is larger than the others and contains dining and recreation facilities including a television lounge, a library, table tennis, a gymnasium, and a music room. The central space has a double-height atrium with provision for a hydroponics facility that has the capacity to provide fresh salad during the dark winter period. Adjacent modules provide science laboratories, offices, workshops, and sleeping areas. The modules all have a unique aerodynamic shape designed to limit snow build-up beneath them.

The standardised modules are constructed from a lightweight steel sub-frame that is transported in one piece to the Antarctic by ship. At their destination they will each be offloaded onto their skis and towed to the site by Caterpillar bulldozers, vehicles that BAS operate at the existing station. Cladding panels are made from glass-reinforced plastic (GRP) enclosing closed cell foam insulation. Floors and internal fittings are also prefabricated.

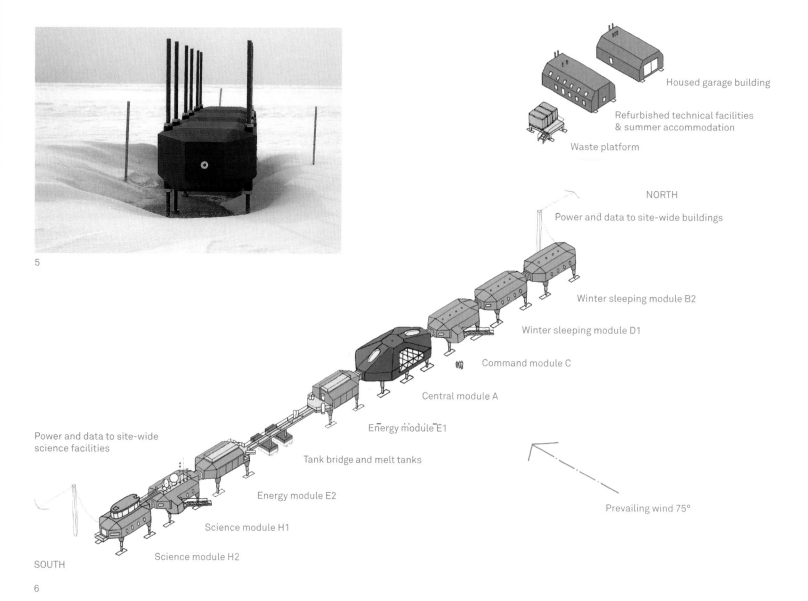

5

Housed garage building

Refurbished technical facilities
& summer accommodation

Waste platform

NORTH

Power and data to site-wide buildings

Winter sleeping module B2

Winter sleeping module D1

Command module C

Central module A

Energy module E1

Power and data to site-wide
science facilities

Tank bridge and melt tanks

Prevailing wind 75°

Energy module E2

Science module H1

SOUTH

Science module H2

6

All elements are fixed mechanically to ensure easy dismantling if there is a need to de-commission the buildings
at the end of their design life. Once the basic shell is
assembled on site and is weather-tight the modules will
be left over winter ready for internal fit-out the following
Austral summer. Many of the internal spaces are made
as fully furnished prefabricated pods that will be transported intact and slotted into place and connected to the
service runs. The standard module weighs 80 tonnes when
fully fitted out. The large central module is expected to
weigh 140 tonnes, which is just within the towing capacity
of the vehicle fleet.

The regular task of lifting the building to prevent it
from becoming buried by the relentless increase in snow
level will be made much easier than in the present station.
It is predicted that three workers will be able to achieve
this task using the mechanical legs in just one week compared to the six who currently do it in an entire season.
The legs can be independently raised by hydraulics and
the snow bulldozed beneath their new position to raise
the entire structure to a higher level.

A combined heat and power diesel generator source
using Aviation Turbine Fuel (AVTUR) that is suitable for
use in very low temperatures will be used to provide power
for heating and air-flow, low energy lighting, and domestic
appliances. The energy modules are interconnected so
that an integrated energy balance can be achieved for
efficiency and reduced environmental impact. In the summer period solar energy will be used to help melt water
when the station capacity is at its maximum. Minimising
water use is crucial because of the energy required to
convert it from snow. The system has therefore been
designed to allow 85 litres per person per day for washing,
showers, flushing (through vacuum aircraft-type toilets),
cooking, and drinking. A sophisticated sewage treatment
plant, waste collection bins, and compactors will ensure
that only the minimum amount of waste is generated
and this will be either incinerated or removed from site.
The disposed grey water, after passing through bioreactor
and a UV unit meets EU bathing standards and so it is
acceptable to discharge it below the ice surface. Components for equipment and fittings are standardised across
the entire facility to reduce the number of spares required.

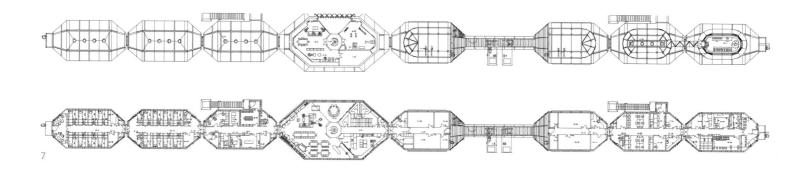

7

8

5 Prototype wind/snow movement testing.
6 Axonometric of the complex layout.
7 Plan at upper and lower level.
8 Testing skid towing system for the
modules – the platform is loaded with
vehicles to the same weight as a module.

Surprisingly, fire is a special risk in Antarctica because of the extremely dry air and consequently a comprehensive fire detection system will be installed along with a water mist suppression system. Nevertheless, the construction was tested to prove that it exceeds British standards and allows all inhabitants to escape safely from a module in an emergency.

Although the designers have integrated extreme build-ing performance criteria into a mobile building strategy the focus has been on reliability and trusted technology rather than pure innovation. Due to its complexity, before any fabrication takes place, all the separate prefabricated elements have been modelled in three-dimensional CAD drawings to ensure there are no services clashes but also to make sure space is used at its optimum efficiency. Services subcontractors are given strict parameters to which they must build their components prior to shipping. This is because of the facility's isolation – it is impossible to send out for broken parts when you are 3,000 kilo-metres south of the Falkland Islands. This remoteness has also been a big factor in making sure the design possesses a sense of comfort and identity for workers who will be isolated for months at a time more than 16,000 kilometres away from the UK. Colour, both internally and externally, has been used to provide variety and personality to the building.

Weatherhaven
BHP Geological Survey Camp

1993–1994
Designer/Constructor: Weatherhaven, Burnaby, Canada
Client: BHP Minerals
Location: Northwest Territories, Canada

Weatherhaven is one of the most experienced providers of shelter buildings for remote locations. The company was founded in Canada in 1981 by the merging of two separate businesses, an expedition organising team and a Vancouver-based construction company. The founders recognised the need for a dedicated approach to the provision of temporary shelter in remote places and developed a strategy to provide a complete service including design, manufacture, packaging, transportation, and erection of buildings, all of which would be created specifically to respond to the logistical problems of remote deployment in harsh environments.

An example of the way in which Weatherhaven operates is the camp deployed to explore the diamond deposits in Canada's remote Northwest Territories. Shortly after their discovery in 1993, a dramatic race ensued to accurately locate deposits and establish operations that would enable commercial extraction processes to begin. The site environment was extremely harsh with only a brief summer period in which to establish base camp. In a race against their competitors, BHP Minerals needed to establish a facility for 110 people and their equipment, which would enable engineering operations to continue throughout the winter.

The first stage of the operation was to establish a Weatherhaven crew shelter so that a construction team could prepare a temporary landing site for heavier aircraft. A single crate was flown in by light aircraft and the building was assembled and in use within four hours. The team then prepared the camp layout, and as the rest of the building components and other equipment were flown in, assembled the entire facility. All the supplies were transported on Douglas DC3 aircraft from Yellow Knife, the capital of the Northwest Territories and the nearest town for many hundreds of miles. The completed facility included sleeping and leisure accommodation, a 24 hour kitchen, showers, and toilets, a hospital, offices, and an engineering base, and was built in 20 working days. Many of the BHP team were able to start work in just a few days as the first buildings became available. Because of the extreme conditions, shelters were required for all the support facilities including water treatment and power supply, and heated corridors between buildings were also used to increase comfort levels and ease operational use.

1 Weatherhaven desert camp utilising
Modular Tenting System (MTS) deployable
shelters for accommodation (rear) and
Deployable Field Ablution systems
(foreground).
2 Expandable remote Site (ERSA)
Hard-walled expandable shelter.
3 Series 8 lightweight deployable
fabric shelter.

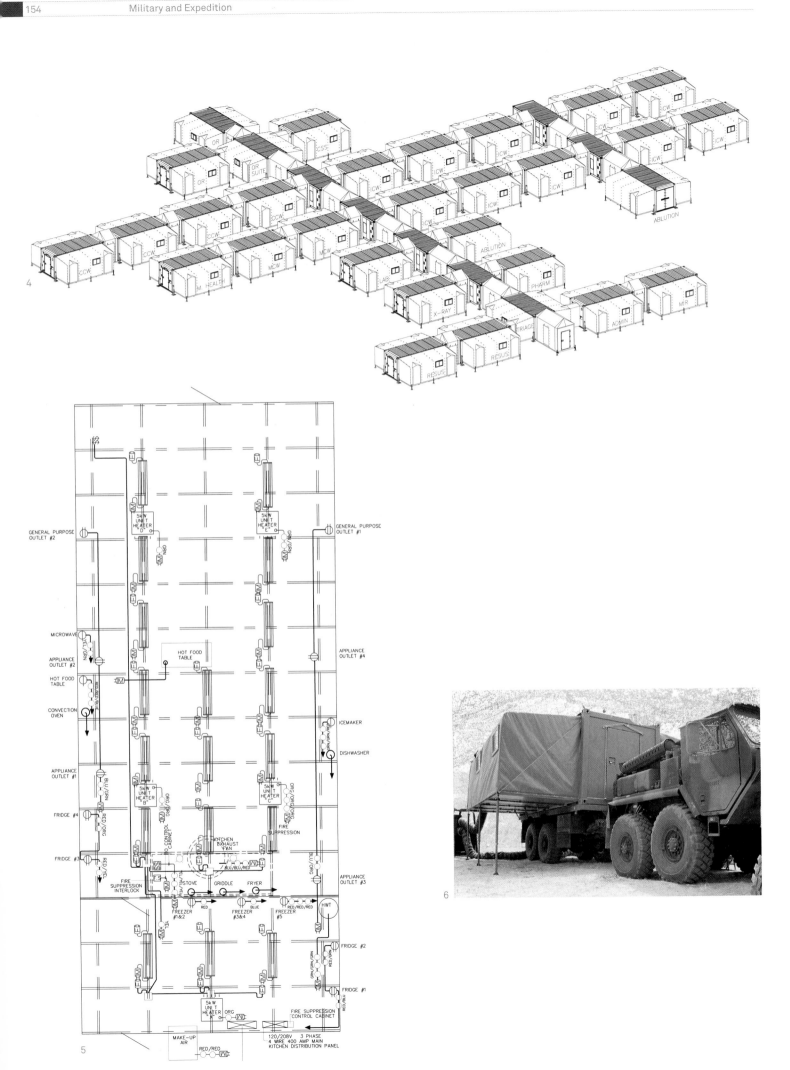

4

5

6

GENERAL PURPOSE
OUTLET #2

5kW
UNIT
HEATER
"D"

5kW
UNIT
HEATER
"E"

GENERAL PURPOSE
OUTLET #1

MICROWAVE

HOT FOOD
TABLE

APPLIANCE
OUTLET #2

APPLIANCE
OUTLET #4

HOT FOOD
TABLE

CONVECTION
OVEN

ICEMAKER

DISHWASHER

APPLIANCE
OUTLET #1

5kW
UNIT
HEATER
"B"

5kW
UNIT
HEATER
"C"

FRIDGE #4

FIRE
SUPPRESSION

FRIDGE #3

KITCHEN
EXHAUST
FAN

FIRE SUPPRESSION
INTERLOCK

STOVE   GRIDDLE   FRYER

APPLIANCE
OUTLET #3

FREEZER
#1&2

FREEZER
#3&4

FREEZER
#5

HWT

FRIDGE #2

FRIDGE #1

5kW
UNIT
HEATER
"A"

FIRE SUPPRESSION
CONTROL CABINET

MAKE-UP
AIR

120/208V   3 PHASE
4 WIRE 400 AMP MAIN
KITCHEN DISTRIBUTION PANEL

4 Camp layout utilising MECC
expandable shelters based on an ISO
shipping container.
5 Typical service layout for a mobile
kitchen shelter.
6 Deploying an MECC from its
transportation.
7 Modular power generation and
servicing unit used with an MECC.
8 Interior of the field ablution unit,
showers on the right.

Weatherhaven provide facilities for a wide range of military and commercial clients but they also deliver humanitarian aid shelter for workers in organisations such as the UN, including living quarters, medical facilities, and logistical workshops. Their products are designed to provide an ingenious practical response to a wide range of problems and they challenge preconceptions about what a building is and what it can do. The Weatherhaven building is a tool that fulfils a functional service upon which not only the success of the operation may depend, but also the lives of its users. Many of the principles involved in their construction are not technologically advanced, neither do they break new ground in terms of materials or techniques. Weatherhaven's design strategies and operation methods are remarkable for their organisational and logistical approach. Though clients can determine the tasks that their operatives will undertake and the location in which they must be based, Weatherhaven draw on their own experience, dedicated research, and product proving to assess shelter requirements and respond with an appropriate building proposal. This is generally in the form of a comprehensive solution – everything from design, materials

sourcing, manufacture, packaging, transportation, and construction services can be provided within the one organisation. They will also assemble, dismantle, and redeploy the facilities if required. Alternatively, as the principles involved in the buildings' erection are very simple, some clients opt to assemble the facility themselves using written and video based instructions.

Formal aesthetic architectural issues are understandably viewed with little importance in Weatherhaven's work. The site impact is of limited duration and often so remote as to be invisible to most of the world. The internal environment of longer-stay remote shelters is, however, of some importance and besides physical comfort, the psychological impact of having communal and leisure space and the opportunity for privacy has been incorporated in the designs. Many of their facilities are used repeatedly, being deployed to different locations in succession, sometimes with varying equipment levels depending on the climate of the area in which they are to be used. The more robust hard shell facilities are returned to Weatherhaven for repair and refurbishment and then redeployed in as-new condition for a further period of service.

Selected Bibliography

'Airtecture Exhibition Hall' in *Detail*, December 1996, pp. 1204, 1274.

'Airtecture: The Festo Exhibition Hall' in *The International Design Magazine*, July/August 1997, pp. 142–143.

'Airtecture' in *Design News*, January 1999, pp. 44–47.

'Air-tecture' in *Space*, December 1998, pp. 163–165.

Ban, Shigeru. *Shigeru Ban*, Laurence King Publishing, London, 2001.

Buchanan, Peter. *Renzo Piano Building Workshop*, vol. II, Phaidon, London, 1993.

Buxton, Pamela. 'Technology on the Move' in *Building Design*, 17th April 2007, pp. 18–20.

Covault, Craig. 'Mars Initiative Leads Station Course Change' in *Aviation Week and Space Technology*, December 1997, pp. 39–40.

Crosbie, Nick. *I'll Keep Thinking*, Black Dog Publishing, London, 2003.

Cunningham, Mark. 'All that Glimmers: The Rolling Stones *Bridges to Babylon* Tour in *SPL*', November 1997, pp. 24–47.

Dalland, Todd. 'Structural Detailing' in *L'Arca* no. 73, July/August 1993.

Dawson, Susan. 'All the World's a Stage' in *The Architect's Journal*, July 10th 1997, pp. 37–39.

Davies, Colin. *The Prefabricated Home*, Reaktion Books, Trowbridge, 2005.

Ellis, Christine. *The History of the Caravan Club*, The Caravan Club Ltd., East Grinstead, 2006.

'Festo's Exhibition Hall' in *World Interior Design (WIND)*, Spring 1997, pp. 34–36.

Furuyama, Masao. *Tadao Ando*, Artemis, Zurich, 1993.

Garbato, Carlo and Mastropietro, Mario (eds.). *Renzo Piano Building Workshop Exhibit Design*, Edizione Lybra Immagine, Milan, 1992.

Glancey, Jonathan. 'Mobile Exhibition Pavilion' in *Architectural Review* no. 1053, November 1984, pp. 70–75.

Goetz, Joachim. 'Architektur mit Muskelspiel' in *Design Report*, January 1997, pp. 52–55.

Goldberger, Paul. *Renzo Piano Buildings and Projects 1971–1989*, Rizzoli, New York, 1989.

Goldsmith, Nicholas. 'The Peripatetic Pavilion' in *Design Quarterly* no. 156, Summer 1992, pp. 28–32.

Gottalier, Tony and Loth, Deborah. 'The Rolling Stones Voodoo Lounge Tour' in *Lighting and Sound International*, September 1994, pp. 64–66.

Harriman, Mark. S. 'Strike up the Bandstand' in *Architecture*, vol. 80, no. 9, September 1991, pp. 102–105.

Herwig, Oliver. *Featherweights: Light, Mobile and Floating Architecture*, Prestel, Munich, 2003.

Holding, Eric. *Mark Fisher: Staged Architecture*, Architectural Monograph no. 52, Wiley-Academy, London, 2000.

'Hot Air' in *Metropolis*, December 1998, pp. 45–47.

'Houses and Aircrafts built with Air' in *Monthly Design*, January 1999, pp. 122–125.

Kennedy, Kriss, J. 'A Horizontal Inflatable Habitat for SEI' in Sadeh, Will, Z., Sture, Stein, Miller, Russell, J. *Engineering, Construction and Operations in Space II, Space '92, Proceedings of the Third International Conference. American Society of Civil Engineers*. New York, 1992, pp. 135–145.

Kronenburg, Robert. *Flexible: Architecture that Responds to Change*, Laurence King Publishing, London, 2007.

Kronenburg, Robert. *FTL: Softness, Movement and Light*, Academy Monograph no. 41, Academy Editions, London, 1997.

Kronenburg, Robert. *Houses in Motion: The History, Development and Potential of the Portable Building* (2nd edition), Wiley-Academy, Chichester, 2002.

Kronenburg, Robert. *Spirit of the Machine: Technology as in Influence on Architectural Form*, Wiley-Academy, Chichester, 2001.

LeCuyer, Annette. *ETFE. Technology and Design*, Birkhäuser, Basel Boston, Berlin, 2008.

Lethby, Mike. 'Babylon Magic: The Stones' Visual Story' in *Live!*, December 1997, pp. 29–33.

'Luftkammer' in *Deutsche Bauzeitschrift (DBZ)*, July 1997.

Lyall, Sutherland. *Rock Sets*, Thames and Hudson, London, 1992.

Melhuish, Clare. 'Go to Work on a Silvery Egg' in *Building Design*, May 27th 1997.

Melhuish, Clare. 'Sets and Drugs and Rock 'n' Roll' in *Building Design*,
May 27th 1994, pp. 16–17.

Melhuish, Clare. 'Snakes Alive' in *Building Design*,
January 20th 1995, pp. 8–9.

Mendell, W.W. (ed.). *The Second Conference on Lunar Bases and Space
Activities in the 21st Century*, NASA. Houston, Texas, 1992.

Meyhöfer, Dirk (ed.). *Contemporary Japanese Architects*,
Taschen, Cologne, 1993.

'Neuartige Traglufthalle mit Luftkammersystem' in *Bautechnik*,
April 1997.

Pawley, Martin. 'Tomorrow's World' in *World Architecture* no. 20,
November 1992, pp. 74–79.

Rice, Peter. *An Engineer Imagines*, Artemis, London, 1994.

Ronconi, Luca (ed.). 'Temporary', *Lotus International*, no. 122,
Milan, November 2004.

Schwartz-Clauss, Mathias (ed.). *Living in Motion: Design
and Architecture for Flexible Dwelling*, Vitra Design Museum,
Weil am Rhein, 2002.

Scrimgeour, Diana. *U2 Show*, Orion, London, 2004.

Siegal, Jennifer (ed.). *Mobile: The Art of Portable Architecture*,
Princeton Architectural Press, New York, 2002.

Slessor, Catherine. 'Pearl of the Orient' in *Architectural Review*,
June 1992, pp. 33–37.

Stein, Karen. D. 'Travelling Show' in *Architectural Record*,
March 1987, pp. 90–93.

Vragnaz, Giovanni. 'Teatro itinerante Karaza' in *Domus*, no. 53,
June 1989, pp. 46–53.

Weatherhaven, Worldwide Logistic Support for Resource Industries.
Weatherhaven Resources Ltd., Burnaby, British Columbia, Canada, 1992.

Index

Illustration Credits

Every effort has been made to trace the copyright holders, architects, and designers and we apologise in advance for any unintentional omission and would be pleased to insert the appropriate acknowledgement in any subsequent edition.